Look,
Think
& Write

Look, Think & Write

Using pictures to stimulate thinking and improve your writing

Hart Day Leavitt
David A. Sohn

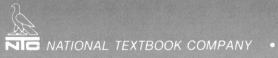

NATIONAL TEXTBOOK COMPANY • Lincolnwood, Illinois

About the Authors

David A. Sohn is Language Arts Chairman, Martin Luther King, Jr. Laboratory School, Evanston, Illinois, and Lecturer, Oakton Community College, Des Plaines, Illinois. He is co-author of *Writing by Doing,* published by National Textbook Company. He has also written several books on film and is the editor of *Ten Top Stories* and *Ten Modern American Short Stories.* In 1984 he received a Governor's Master Teacher Award from the State of Illinois.

Hart Day Leavitt is Lecturer in English Composition at Tufts University. He has taught Freshman Composition at Harvard University and for many years was a member of the English Department at Phillips Andover Academy. He is the originator of the *Stop, Look, & Write* series and has written widely in the field of English Composition.

Acknowledgments

The authors wish to acknowledge the help and support of Leonard Fiddle, Gay Menges, Toni Burbank, Jean Highland, and Ned Leavitt in the development and editing of this book.

Excerpts from the following works were reprinted with permission of the authors or publishers.

Annie Dillard, *Pilgrim at Tinker Creek,* New York: Bantam Books, 1975, p. 6.

John D. MacDonald, *One Fearful Yellow Eye.* Greenwich, Conn.: Fawcett Gold Medal Book, 1966, p. 7.

Shirley MacLaine, *Don't Fall Off the Mountain,* New York: Bantam Books, 1971, p. 87.

Joyce Maynard, "When Young Stops Being Young," *Mademoiselle,* Oct., 1976, p. 174.

Tom Wolfe, *The Kandy-Kolored Tangerine-Flake Streamline Baby.* New York: Noonday Press, 1969, pp. 146-147.

Photographs are credited on pages 226-231.

Book Design: Karen Christoffersen

Contents

Introduction

Everyone can learn to write better — that's what this book is all about. To be a good writer, you must be awake, alert, aware, and observant. *Look, Think & Write* is based upon the idea that to write well, you must study your world with a precise eye and interpret what you see with accuracy and imagination. By showing you how much there is to see in a picture, this book will help you become more observant and more skillful at writing about what you see.

Look, Think & Write is not just a book of pictures. It is a book about pictures, about language, and about thinking. One of the main reasons for using photographs and other visuals to stimulate writing is to emphasize particular details. The writing exercises and opportunities in this book will help you find ways to express meaning in the most effective possible ways. This "meaning" is the result of observation, and must include the **particular,** the **specific,** the **detail.** The soft, vague words and old abstractions such as *good, neat, wonderful,* and *nice* are futile and foggy for writing that focuses on clarity and forceful imagery.

Good writers differ from one another in style, in the forms they use, and in the ways in which they see the world. They all do *see* the world. They notice everything. They observe the shapes and colors of nature, the sounds of city streets, the smells of a country kitchen. They watch the tiny movements of people's eyes and fingers. They listen to the ways in which people talk when they feel angry, afraid, or happy. Nothing is too small or too large to escape their attention. Like Sherlock Holmes, Nero Wolfe, and other great detectives of fiction, they develop the skills of observation until they become second nature.

If you work at writing and use the various sections of this book for practice, your steady, daily efforts will lead you to notice more in the world around you and to think more about what you see. You will face a blank sheet of paper with confidence and find that writing can be fun because you will have strengthened your skills, your imagination, and your ease with words.

This book is based upon a technique that was conceived by Hart Day Leavitt in his many composition classes. An earlier version of this book was published as *Stop, Look & Write* and sold nearly a million copies in several editions. It has now been considerably revised and improved. The larger format, the addition of numerous specific assignments, and the new, exciting photographs and other visuals have enhanced and strengthened the book. *Look, Think & Write* is a new, better, and stronger program for learning to observe and to improve writing skills.

The addition of the word *think* to the new title is very important. To write effectively, one has to think and interpret experience clearly and to transform observations and thoughts into clear words. Critical thinking, then, is the heart of the writing process.

Anne Morrow Lindbergh once wrote, "Writing is thinking. It is more than living, for it is being conscious of living." And it was Ralph Waldo Emerson who pointed out that "nature and books belong to eyes that see them." These two observations illustrate what this book intends: to help you to become a better writer through learning to see clearly and accurately and to transform what you see into writing that will communicate your thinking with clarity and style. With a serious attitude, regular practice, and concentrated work, you can achieve these goals.

The Image of Concentration 1

The pictures in this section were selected to dramatize concentration. In them we see people focusing intensely upon something.

Concentration is the ability to focus the mind upon a problem or task. Words associated with concentration are *observation, vigilance, watching, alertness, diligence, inspection, study,* and *attention.* Deep concentration is one of the most difficult skills to learn, for all distractions must be ignored and the mind must be focused fully and alertly upon the object of attention.

Although it may be difficult to concentrate well, it is one of the most rewarding skills one can learn. A person who can concentrate intently possesses one of those qualities that can make the difference between success and failure in a job or a role. Successful scientists, detectives, surgeons, pilots, artists, musicians, and chefs are all examples of people who focus upon a task with energy and persistence. A good writer is one who watches, listens, and concentrates.

In preparation for the writing exercises, study each picture with the same close concentration you can see in the photographs. What does concentration look like?

Exercises for Writing

1. For each picture, list three details that show the concentration.

2. Select the picture that interests you most. Now try to visualize what is going on outside the picture by answering these questions in a paragraph.

    a. What is going on? What are the people saying, thinking?

    b. What might be the cause of this intense moment?

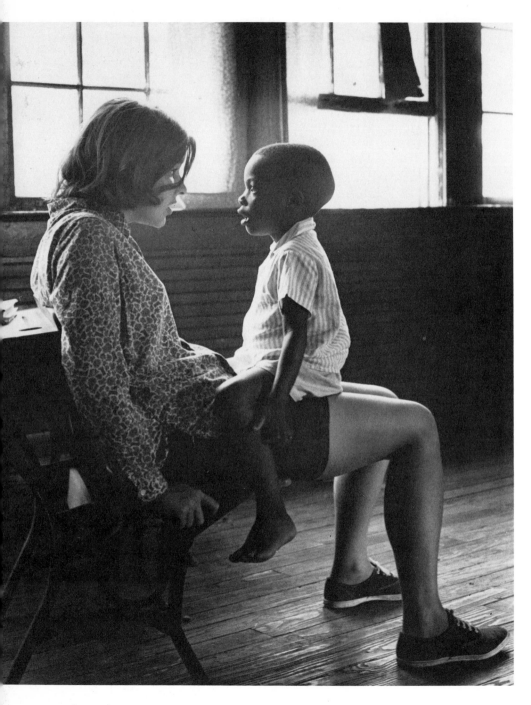

3

On Your Own

1. Study any simple object (a fork, for instance) for at least five minutes. As you observe it, list all the details you can about the object — size, shape, color, texture, design, and so on. When you have completed your list, write a paragraph that describes the object so clearly that the reader could pick this particular object out of a group of similar objects (*this* fork out of a tray of ten forks, for instance).

2. Observe a person for two or three minutes. Concentrate on making a detailed mental photograph. Then, without looking back at the person, write a list of as many details as you can about that person — facial features, makeup, clothing, colors, jewelry, posture, movements, etc. Now check your list by looking back at that person. Did you miss anything? Were you wrong about anything?

3. Study a painting or photograph in a magazine of one or two persons. List all the details you see in the picture — colors, shapes, facial expressions, background. Write a paragraph that describes the picture so the reader can see it.

Summary

Most people do not fully concentrate when they observe and study other people and events. Concentration demands energy, purpose, and patience. It is frequently surprising to discover how much you miss with a first glance. When you observe, concentrate!

> *Perception is attention.*
> —Novalis

2

How Much Do You Really See?

All the pictures and exercises in this section have been selected to train you to see and write with greater precision and accuracy. In these pictures there are masses of data: objects, faces, gestures, clothes, buildings, expressions, actions, relationships, and odd combinations. Seeing it all requires intense concentration.

A valuable prewriting technique for managing such masses of data is to create a detail list. This is a procedure often used by professional writers in preparing to write magazine articles and by students preparing for long essays.

Creating a detail list of observations and information is like filling the memory bank of a computer with data. Once the raw data is stored in the memory bank, the programmer can use it to solve problems. Similarly, the detail list can provide the writer with the raw material for an interesting composition.

Study the picture on page 9. A detail list for this picture might include physical details, facial expressions, gestures of hands, and reactions of people to what is happening.

Here is an example of a detail list for page 9.

- hands clenching, holding, covering up, in pockets, hanging
- boy looks puzzled
- almost all mouths shut, two or three open
- little girl and soldier in middle leaning
- some standing very stiff
- one man looking at another
- sharp contrasts everywhere in style and attitude
- three skirts the same
- knobby knees

Spend five minutes adding items to this detail list. When you are finished, exchange your list with a classmate. What did you miss? How many things were you able to add to the original detail list?

Study the following passage from "The Last American Hero" by the journalist Tom Wolfe. It shows precise, important, and thorough observation.

And suddenly there's a big roar from behind, down in the infield, and then I see one of the great sights in stock car racing. That infield! The cars have been piling into the infield by the hundreds, parking in there on the clay and the grass, every which way, angled down and angled up, this way and that, where the ground is uneven, these beautiful blazing brand-new cars with the sun exploding off the windshields and the baked enamel and the glassy lacquer, hundreds, thousands of cars stacked this way and that in the infield with the sun bolting down and no shade, none at all, just a couple of Coca-Cola stands out there. And already the good old boys and girls are out beside the cars, with all these beautiful little buds in short shorts already spread-eagled out on top of the car roofs, pressing down on good hard slick automobile sheet metal, their little cupcake bottoms aimed up at the sun. . . .

And everybody, good old boys and girls of all ages, are out there with portable charcoal barbecue ovens set up, and folding tubular steel terrace furniture, deck chairs and things, and Thermos jugs and coolers full of beer—and suddenly it is not the upcountry South at all but a concentration of the modern suburbs, all jammed into that one space, from all over America, with blazing cars and instant goodies, all cooking under the bare blaze—inside a strange bowl.

—Tom Wolfe

Exercises for Writing

1. Using your detail list, write a composition based on the crowd scene on page 9. Answer an important question. What are they watching? Describe the crowd. How are they reacting to what they see? Use specific examples from the picture to illustrate your points.

2. Write a paragraph about the picture on page 10, using a detail list as a basis for your writing. Explain the situation in this picture with your details.

3. Create a detail list for the picture on page 11. Using your list, describe this scene as clearly as possible in a paragraph or more.

4. Create a detail list for the picture on page 12. Identify three clusters or groups of details which seem to fit together. Then write a paragraph or more about the picture using one cluster of details.

12

On Your Own

1. Choose a scene from your life that interests you and observe it for 15 minutes. Use a notebook to list all the details you can see in the scene. Some possible places are:

- a library
- a restaurant
- a cafeteria
- a street corner
- a park

2. Study one of the following. List all the details you can find in the room. Concentrate. Be accurate.

- one of your classrooms
- a living room
- your bedroom

3. Study a closet (not your own). List all the details you observe in the closet. Think of the closet as a collection of clues about the people who use it. Write two to three paragraphs about what the closet suggests to you, based upon the details.

Summary

You may have discovered that learning to observe carefully is not a simple task if you do it well. You must concentrate and try not to miss anything. Good writers are keen observers. They see not only the whole picture but also the small details that create the picture.

Continue to work seriously on observation and concentration as you use this book. Your efforts will be rewarded as your writing improves and you create more lively, specific compositions.

> *I do not understand;*
> *I pause; I examine—*
> —Montaigne

The Power of Observation

3

Most pictures are visual compositions that use the arrangement of details to create a single effect. Constructing detail lists helps you to analyze the elements that create this effect.

Written compositions also create a single effect that is generally suggested by the title and stated more fully as the main idea in the topic sentence of a paragraph or, in compositions of several photographs, in the thesis statement.

The topic sentence serves to state the main idea and to promise the reader more information about that idea. Usually that promise is found in a word or phrase that states the writer's attitude toward the main idea. Here is an example of a topic sentence for a paragraph about the picture on page 18.

Two very different actions are going on in this exciting scene from a bullfight.

In the example above, the main idea is "two actions in this picture," and the attitude is "different."

Exercises for Writing

1. Give each picture in this section a good title. Your title should express the main idea of the situation in an interesting way.

2. Write a paragraph about the picture on page 18. Use the topic sentence stated above.

3. What is happening in the picture on page 19? Write one sentence that describes the dramatic action in the picture. List the details that contribute to the dramatic action.

4. Study the picture of the three girls on page 20 and decide what the situation might be that explains the facial expressions in the photograph. Write one sentence that states the main idea of the picture. List the details that contribute to the main idea.

5. Write one sentence that states your interpretation of the picture on page 21. You should produce a good topic sentence that states an attitude suitable for development into a paragraph. After you have created your topic sentence, write the entire paragraph.

6. Read the following student-written paragraph about the picture on page 20. Does it contain a good topic sentence that states the main idea and the writer's attitude? If not, write a good topic sentence. Next, identify any details that do not pertain to the main idea. Now rewrite the paragraph beginning with the topic sentence and arranging the supporting details in an appropriate order.

> The three girls are quite cute in the way they are dressed. Their sophisticated costumes contrast with their youthful innocence. They are also cute in the way they express their nervousness. The one on the left is staring vaguely and making a facial expression which she would definitely avoid making if she could see herself. The middle one, with her hand over her mouth, gives the impression of being shocked at the size of the audience. I think rather that she is just nervously scratching her nose because she should not be able to see the audience since she is not on stage yet. Of course she might be shocked at seeing only a part of the crowd or at having her picture taken. The one on the right has assumed a very dignified face. The photograph emphasizes the contrast in the manner in which each girl expresses her nervousness. The photograph shows not only how out of place children are when acting in a serious play, but also how cute they are in the process.

7. The picture on page 22 shows a very unusual situation. An entire story could be written about this scene. Write one sentence that suggests how this situation might have happened. Write a sentence good enough to introduce the story. Write the story.

8. Select the one picture that interests you the most and study it carefully. Write a main idea (thesis) sentence to begin a paragraph. Now write at least a paragraph based upon the situation and the details in the picture.

9. Read the following words of Helen Keller, then write a composition showing how your life would change if you lost the senses she writes about in her essay.

The Seeing See Little

> Only the deaf appreciate hearing; only the blind realize the manifold blessings that lie in sight. Particularly does this observation apply to those who have lost sight and hearing in adult life. But those who have never suffered

impairment of sight or hearing seldom make the fullest use of these blessed faculties. Their eyes and ears take in all sights and sounds hazily, without concentration, and with little appreciation. It is the same old story of not being grateful for what we have until we lose it, of not being conscious of health until we are ill.

I have often thought it would be a blessing if each human being were stricken blind and deaf for a few days at some time during his or her early adult life. Darkness would make people more appreciative of sight; silence would teach them the joys of sound.

Now and then I have tested my seeing friends to discover what they *see*. Recently I was visited by a very good friend who had just returned from a long walk in the woods, and I asked her what she had observed. "Nothing in particular," she replied. I might have been incredulous had I not been accustomed to such responses, for long ago I became convinced that the seeing see little.

If I were the president of a university, I should establish a compulsory course in "How to Use Your Eyes." The professor would try to show the pupils how they could add joy to their lives by really seeing what passes unnoticed before them. He or she would try to awake their dormant and sluggish faculties.

I who am blind can give one hint to those who see—one admonition to those who would make full use of the gift of sight: Use your eyes as if tomorrow you would be stricken blind. And the same method can be applied to the other senses. Hear the music of voices, the song of a bird, the mighty strains of an orchestra, as if you would be sricken deaf tomorrow. Touch each object you want to touch as if tomorrow your tactile sense would fail. Smell the perfume of flowers, taste with relish each morsel, as if tomorrow you could never smell or taste again. Make the most of every sense; glory in all the facets of pleasure and beauty that the world reveals to you through the several means of contact that Nature provides. But of all the senses, I am sure that sight must be the most delightful.

Three Days to See, Doubleday and Co., © 1933

—Helen Keller

18

20

On Your Own

1. Find three good pictures from a magazine. Express the main idea for each picture in an effective title.

2. Select one picture from the three magazine pictures. Write a paragraph that supports the main idea with details.

3. Framing a scene: Cut out a one-inch square from the center of a 3×5 file card. Find a scene full of details that interests you. Hold the file card six inches from your eyes and look through the hole. You have framed an area. Write all the details you see through the square. Describe the scene viewed through the square in one paragraph. Does the scene have a main idea? If so, state it in your first sentence. Give the paragraph an effective title.

Summary

A keen observer is not satisfied with a mere glance. The curious observer carefully examines the environment, always looking for interesting material and fresh observations. The effective writer looks, studies, examines, and searches for good material to interpret. Observe daily life with sharp eyes and keen senses.

> *It is a world to see.*
> —John Lyly

4

Form and Size

When you are observant, you notice sizes, outlines, depth, roundness, length, squareness, and other forms; and you can describe an object in itself, or as a part of a whole place, person, or scene.

First, you must see and feel the effects of physical forms, then you can express them in words and phrases that are literally accurate and also suggest the mood. The following passage describes several physical forms and also strongly suggests a mood.

> ... from the southwest, a wall of fog had advanced upon his ship. Great convolutions of vapours flew over, swirling about masts and funnel, which looked as if they were going to melt .... There was another ship near—a mere blot on the fog's brightness.
>
> —from "The Tale" by Joseph Conrad

Notice how the writer compares the existing shapes to other objects in order to further enhance the mood: *wall, looked as if they were going to melt, blot.*

The picture on page 27 is obviously comparing two skeletons. Read the following paragraph written by a student. Notice that the writer studied the picture, determined the main idea, and observed how form and size work together to achieve the effect of contrast.

> The two skeletons were on a revolving platform, and the camera waited until they were sideways to emphasize the neat, small curves of the man's head, as against the awkward, boulder-like skull of the ape. Also the big bulbous bone-cage of the ape looked gross and out of balance next to the man's ribs, which are tighter and lighter.
>
> —from a student essay

Exercises for Writing

1. In the picture on page 27 imagine that you are one skeleton talking to the other. Describe yourself as you looked when you were alive. Include details such as your shape when you had flesh on your bones.

2. Describe three different shapes in the picture of the elephant on page 28.

3. Imagine you are the elephant in the picture on page 28. Describe your physical features to the world and tell why you think you are beautiful.

4. Write one sentence that describes the shape of the experimental house pictured on page 29.

5. You are the architect who designed the house pictured on page 29. Explain why you think its shape makes it a lovely house and a wonderful place to live.

6. Study the picture on page 30. You are the fighter who lost the fight. In a paragraph describe the shape of your face after the fight as you look into the mirror. Be sure you state the main idea and mood first, then explain through the use of details.

7. Select one picture and write a series of separate sentences describing several of the most prominent shapes. Then put them together to make a brief, united paragraph. Relate the parts so they flow in a sensible sequence.

One way to organize such a description is to arrange the details according to patterns in the picture. In the picture of the skeletons, for example, the chest bones of the two figures form a pattern of lines and forms that could be compared together in a series of sentences. Similarly, there are patterns in the two skulls.

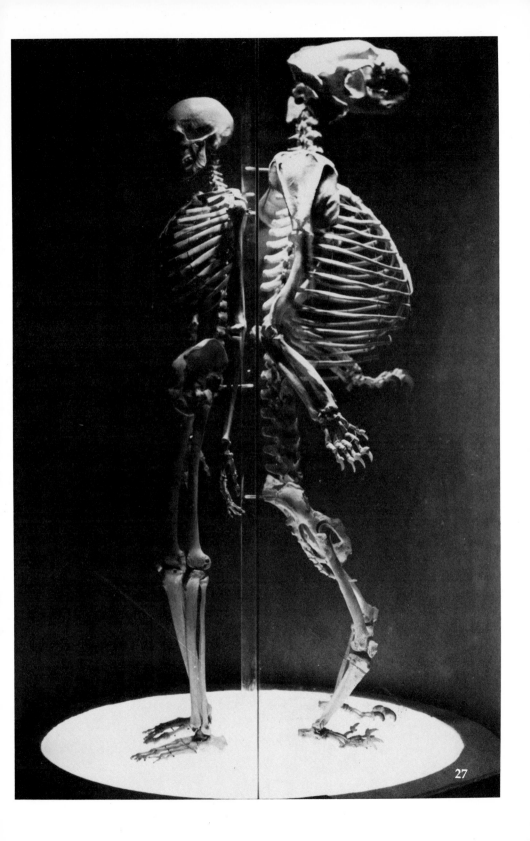

27

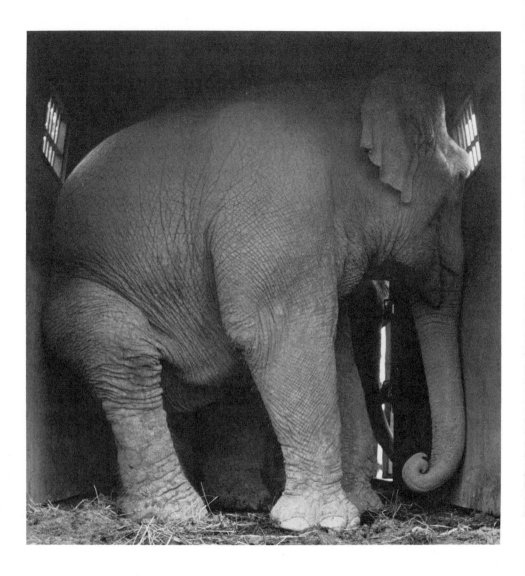

30

On Your Own

1. Sit in a room, a courtyard, or another place. List the shapes you observe. Describe them clearly. Find as many as you possibly can.

2. Study the sky on a day when there are clouds in it. Describe the shapes of the clouds. What do they resemble?

3. Select an animal to observe. Study it. Describe it in terms of shapes — the nose, the ears, the legs, and other features.

4. Select a person to study. Observe the person's face. Describe the hair, eyes, nose, mouth, and total face in terms of shapes.

5. Locate three objects in your home that have unusual shapes. Write a riddle for each of the objects by describing the object without naming it. Be sure that you write the riddle so clearly that the reader or listener can picture it. Then see if the reader or listener can guess what it is.

Summary

Visual relationships are based on forms and shapes. You can see most things in terms of circles, squares, triangles, and other combinations of lines.

Begin to see people, objects, plants, and structures in terms of shapes. Architects, designers, painters, sculptors, writers, and other artists give form to raw material. We shape our own lives. Give thought to the roles that shapes and forms play in your life.

> *Art is nothing without form.*
> —Gustave Flaubert

> *Form ever follows function.*
> —Louis Henri Sullivan

Appeal to the Senses

5

When you describe, you try to create through words the mood or spirit of places, actions, persons, animals, or objects. You are using words to transmit a picture and a mood to the reader.

The writer must use concrete and exact words that appeal to the senses, create atmosphere, and suggest sharp images. *Drudgery* is much more effective than *a lot of work*. *Slime* creates a sharper picture than *dirty water*. *Smash* or *pummel* are more effective than *hit*.

Here are sensory words that appeal to the five senses.

Vague		**Effective**
Sound:	talk	chatter, mumble, whisper, scream
Touch:	feel	fumble, grab, grope, stroke
Sight:	beautiful	stunning, dazzling, shimmering, sparkling
Taste:	bad	rancid, putrid, vile, rotten
Smell:	bad	decayed, pungent, spoiled, mildewed

When you create images through words, avoid clichés such as *smart as a whip,* or *sky blue.* Clichés are worn-out expressions that lack effectiveness because they have been used millions of times. If the word picture comes easily, it might well be a cliché.

A thesaurus can help you to choose a specific word that fits your thinking better than a vague one. Remember, however, that no two words mean exactly the same thing. Pay careful attention to what you see, hear, touch, taste, smell, and feel, and develop your vocabulary of sensory words to use in your writing.

To better understand the difference between a vague and a specific statement, compare the following original sentences with their revised versions.

Original: As the first child in the family, I have always felt *kind of different.*

Revised: As the first child in the family, I have often felt *untidy and clumsy, like a visitor.*

Original: Neither group, athletes or scholars, wants to mix with the other. Much of *this* has to do with lack of communication.

Revised: Neither group, athletes or scholars, wants to mix with the other. Much of *this isolation* has to do with lack of communication.

Original: (Looking at the picture on page 36) The old woman *could care less about her food.*

Revised: Shoko, the elderly seamstress, listlessly whisked the morsel of tuna into her mouth as she met the weariness of the day's end.

The following examples show how sharp, sensuous language creates the mood of what the writer saw and felt.

> When Caesar refused the crown the third time, the rabblement clapped their chopped hands, and threw up their sweaty night-caps, and uttered such a deal of stinking breath that it almost choked Caesar . . . and I durst not laugh for fear of opening my lips and receiving the bad air.
> —Casca in Shakespeare's *Julius Caesar*

> Around the Indian campfire, the yellow light flickers on small children, heavy with silver and turquoise for the occasion, playing in the dust. The light exposes the thin, starved form of a dog sneaking into the circle to snap at a discarded bone and disappearing into the night.
> —from a student essay

When you choose sensory words to create sharp images in your writing, pay attention to the connotations of words. The connotation of a word is the overtone of feeling, the personal definition that a person attaches to the word in addition to its dictionary meaning (denotation). *Thin, skinny,* and *slender* have the same denotation but very different connotations. If someone used one of these three words to describe you, which would you prefer?

Although it is technically true that no word has the same meaning to any two people because all have had different personal experiences, a writer cannot attend to all of the subtle differences in connotation. However, it is crucial that a writer be sensitive to connotative meanings that an audience might attach to certain words and phrases. Some words carry strong sexist, racial, ethnic, or social overtones of meaning, either positive or negative. Such words as *girl, youngster, cute, radical,* or *ward boss* are loaded with emotional meanings.

Three good rules to remember are: avoid slang unless you are writing for a specific audience and you are very current about their language; be careful in using a thesaurus — it does not distinguish differences in connotation; and pay attention — listen — to the users of your language. Learn to distinguish connotative meanings of words in addition to their denotative meanings.

Exercises for Writing

1. Review the pictures in this section, concentrating on precise details. Now, invent sharp, clear, original phrases that will make the reader stop, look, and think.

2. Study the picture of the runners on page 38. Write a paragraph that creates this picture for the reader with sensory language. Begin with a good topic sentence that states the mood.

3. Describe the tree on page 40 in a piece of writing that conveys the shape, details, and impact of the scene.

4. Pick one of the photographs in this section and write a fully developed paragraph describing the details that create the mood of the picture. Study the image accurately and choose words carefully to avoid clichés.

On Your Own

1. Watch a television commercial for food or drink. Write down the descriptive words that are used to encourage viewers to buy the product.

2. Study three ads from magazines. List as many sensory words as you can from the ads.

3. From actual life, choose an object or an event that conveys a distinct feeling or spirit — fear, craziness, tension, speed, romance, defeat, grief, and so on. In an organized paragraph describe the object or event with details suggesting the feeling.

4. Choose something from your personal life — a room you love, clothes you hate, a place you remember nostalgically, an object you like to play with, or a tense, difficult person. Try to sense the details of your subject in your mind. Now describe it in writing so that the reader can both see the person or object and also understand how you feel about it.

Summary

Good writers know the value of sensory words for creating word pictures that are vivid. As you read stories, novels, and poetry, notice how writers use vivid words to make their pictures come alive. Collect sensory words and use them in your writing.

Painting is silent poetry, and poetry,
painting that speaks.
—Plutarch

Moving
Word Pictures 6

The exercises in this section present a special problem: creating and suggesting motion through language. For this purpose, the best words are concrete and active. Readers object to passive verbs, like *was heard* and *had been taken,* or inactive verbs like almost all forms of *to be,* because their action, if any, is impersonal and backward. Compare these two statements about the motion of a baseball.

- The ball came at me.
- The ball whizzed (shot or flew) right at my eyes.

Even active verbs can sometimes be ineffective, such as verbs like *go, use, act,* and *take.* Although they do convey some sense of movement, they are too soft and general to make a memorable impression. Much better are verbs like *race, poke, mince,* and *snatch* — as long as you don't use too many of them too often. Such words create a sharp picture of a specific movement unlike other movements.

Or, you can go further, choosing phrases, clauses, and other combinations of words that run together to convey a sense of the motions happening in swift sequence. The following is a part of Shirley MacLaine's description of coming to a big Hollywood party.

> Then you hear her coming toward the reception hall—your hostess, her Paris heels clicking across inlaid wooden floors, and her petticoats swishing under a skirt of exactly the correct length. *A brilliant pair of diamond clusters spill from her ears just below her coifed hair.* She is well aware of their blinding magnificence, never forgetting what she paid for them as she smiles a charming but empty smile and with a wave of patronizing grandeur compliments you on your costume jewelry. . . . *Then you get sucked into the greetings, the sweeping, larger-than-life greetings, with "Dahhhlings" and hugs and anticipated pecks on your cheeks.* You feel the women draw back slightly for fear a smudge of lipstick will mar their carefully studied makeups.
> —from *Don't Fall Off the Mountain* by Shirley MacLaine

The following passage describes an entirely different kind of motion, but with the same devices of language.

> The motion of the ship was extravagant. *Her lurches had an appalling helplessness: she pitched as if taking a header into a void, and seemed to find a wall to hit every time.* When she rolled she fell on her side headlong, and she would be righted back by such a demolishing blow that Jukes felt her reeling as a clubbed man reels before he collapses. The gale howled and scuffled about gigantically in the darkness, as though the entire world were one black gully. *At certain moments the air streamed against the ship as if sucked through a tunnel with a concentrated solid force of impact that seemed to lift her clean out of the water and keep her up for an instant with only a quiver running through her from end to end.* And then she would begin her tumbling again as if dropped back into a boiling cauldron.
>
> —from *Typhoon* by Joseph Conrad

To write accurately and suggestively, you first have to watch motion and sense its mood. Or, as in imaginative fiction, you have to see the motion in your imagination and feel it as if it were happening to you.

As a way to get started, many writers use the technique of *freewriting*. This is like the warm-up exercises in a sport. To freewrite, put the point of your pen or pencil on the paper and start writing the first words, phrases, or ideas you think of, even if they turn out to be nonsense. Keep writing for five minutes or so without stopping.

Another version of this technique is *focused freewriting*. Begin by selecting a topic: football, home, telephone. Now begin writing with the first word or phrase or idea you think of and keep on writing for at least five minutes, even if you get far away from your original topic. Chances are you will have discovered something worth expanding in a paragraph or composition. If not, keep freewriting.

Exercises for Writing

1. Study each picture in this section. Write a sentence about each picture that describes the motion involved and the feeling transmitted by the picture.

2. Select one picture in this section. Write a paragraph that describes the picture in more detail. Use a topic sentence to state the main idea.

3. To challenge your skills, write imitations of the four italicized sentences in the examples on pages 43 and 44. Use words as exact as those in the originals but describe the opposite feeling. For example, instead of MacLaine's picture of phoniness, make the hostess an honest, direct person. Instead of Conrad's violent storm, make the seas smooth.

4. Select the picture that interests you most. Freewrite for five minutes about the motions in the picture. Write a paragraph built around something that surfaced about the picture in your freewriting. Use specific verbs wherever appropriate to convey the motions in the picture.

49

On Your Own

1. Find a good thesaurus in a bookstore or library. If possible, purchase one. A good thesaurus is one of the most useful tools for a writer. List the words that are variations for *walk* and *run*. Notice the difference in both the denotation and connotations of the words.

2. Study people in motion. Describe at least five people in five different sentences without using the words *walk, run* or *dance*.

3. Using good motion words, describe a five minute action sequence from a film or television show.

4. Read through a newspaper. Find at least ten good motion words in the news stories, sports page, or other sections of the paper. List them.

5. Study the following motions. Create an original way of communicating the sense of movement for each. For example, the cat flowed smoothly and quietly toward the bird, soundless and deadly.

- a car skidding
- a friend's peculiar habit
- a cat stalking a bird
- a car coming at you too fast
- a football player avoiding a tackle
- a fishing rod bending as a fish runs with the line
- a policeman trying to hurry a slow driver
- someone at a meeting trying to get attention
- a water skier swinging out on an arc

6. Find a vivid verb to replace the verb in each of the following sentences.

 a. The crowd made noise when the soccer team won the game.

 b. Maria did not like the steak and vegetables at the restaurant.

 c. Herman did poorly on the test.

 d. Hyung hurried to the theater to be on time for the movie.

 e. Janine threw the ball to first base.

 f. Tiffany liked to play cards.

Summary

So much of life and art relates to movement. Learning to use specific, vivid verbs is one of the most valuable skills a writer can learn. When you read stories, novels, poetry, and nonfiction, read with an awareness of how well the writer uses motion words. Avoid soft, vague words. Use sharp, accurate verbs to describe action in your sentences.

> *The poetry of motion.*
> —Kenneth Grahame

Discovering Similarities

7

Up to this point, you have been learning to observe with concentration and precision. The more you see clearly, the more you will have to write about. As you pay closer attention to whatever you encounter, your writing will become more accurate and interesting. You can *show* the reader what you want to communicate.

Beginning with this section, you will be asked to consider other aspects of subject matter and find more extensive substance for your writing. In this section, in addition to details, you will begin to look for relationships and connections. The more you connect facts and ideas, the more you will have to say.

In this section you will explore similarities between pairs of pictures. As you compare each of the following pairs of pictures, you will be training yourself to find likenesses among people, objects, actions, gestures, clothes, expressions, moods, ideas, and attitudes.

Consider this statement about the pictures on pages 58 and 59. It states a similarity that could be described at some length in a paragraph:

> These two women, one a nurse, the other a Geisha, look
> as if they were acting a part they didn't want to play.

When you compare two things, you examine them to discover the likenesses or similarities they share. If you were asked to compare a leopard and a cat, for example, you would quickly see several basic resemblances between them. There are also differences that you notice, but your goal in this chapter is to search for comparisons — ways in which things resemble each other. The next chapter will discuss contrasts, which is the word for differences.

These words are synonyms for similarities: *likenesses, resemblances, analogies, relationships, comparisons,* and *connections.* The words *simile* and *metaphor* stand for figures of speech that compare two things with words. Similes and metaphors will be discussed in a future chapter. With the following pages, focus your attention upon detecting comparisons.

Exercises for Writing

1. Compare the two people in the picture on page 57. List all the ways in which they are similar.

2. Study the pictures on pages 58 and 59. Although these are two individuals, how are their expressions similar? What similar thoughts may they be thinking? Write a short piece of writing comparing these two people.

3. Study the pictures on pages 60 and 61. List the similarities in these pictures in terms of:

- clothing
- posture
- action
- expression
- mood

4. Write a paragraph that shows how the feelings of the people in the pictures on pages 62 and 63 are similar.

5. Here is a detailed list of comparisons about the pair of pictures on pages 64 and 65:

- both figures are off the ground
- in both pictures the legs of the figures are apart
- the backgrounds are still and impersonal
- both figures are isolated
- in each picture a foot is prominent
- some danger is possible in both pictures
- the reasons for these actions may be the same

What can you add to the list? Study the pictures carefully and write two or three paragraphs using this list (and your own), emphasizing the similarities between the two pictures.

6. Select one pair of pictures and write a composition that emphasizes the likenesses they share.

On Your Own

Here are the beginnings of several student essays based on important similarities the writer has seen or read about. Read these in preparation for doing the following exercises.

> Both Karen Silkwood and Billy Budd were rebels who were destroyed by the very thing they rebelled against.
>
> The behavior of youth in the past 15 years is very much like the way youth behaved in the 1920s. In both periods, people in their teens and early twenties suddenly became very open and uninhibited, shying away from the strong influences of the other generation. In short, they did what they pleased.

1. In preparation for a composition describing a similarity you have observed in actual life, study the following list of areas of similarities among people and add other items to the list.

- physical characteristics
- emotions
- ideas
- actions
- personality traits

2. Find two people who differ a great deal in personality, size, age, and other characteristics. List the ways in which they are alike. Write a composition in which you point out that although they are very different people, they are alike in several ways.

3. Study two commercials (for different products). List the similarities. Then write a paragraph that describes the similarities.

4. Compare one school subject with another. For example, compare mathematics with history, or science with music. How are they alike? Write a composition in which you compare the two subjects you select.

5. Write a composition in which you compare a sad movie with a comedy.

6. Compare each of the following pairs. First, write a list of the likenesses for each pair. Then select one of the pairs and write at least a paragraph that shows how the subjects of the pair are similar.

- a whale and a goldfish
- a teacher and a student
- a cat and a leopard
- an automobile and a bus
- a movie theater and a television set
- a referee and a football player
- a potato and an orange

Summary

The art and the skills of comparison are very important for the effective writer. Two things which seem very different usually have some similar qualities. As you observe, notice likenesses wherever possible. Such an attitude will sharpen your observation and will help you to find raw material which may, at first, seem useless.

> *Learn, compare, collect the facts.*
> —Ivan Pavlov

Discovering Differences

8

This section will explore contrasts (differences). Contrast almost always begins with similarity. When you contrast a dog with a cat, you discover certain basic similarities immediately. Both live, breathe, and exist through consuming food. Both are often pets. Once you have found basic likenesses, you can analyze the differences between a dog and a cat. The more similar the objects, the more subtle and interesting the differences.

Because contrast begins with finding similarities, the process is frequently called comparison and contrast. When you are asked to contrast, note the similarities first, then look for the differences.

Writing about similarities and differences takes careful planning because the writer is presenting many details and two points of view. It is useful to begin with two detail lists — one of similarities and one of differences.

Next, group related items in each detail list. For example, if you are contrasting living in the country with living in the city, you would group items about social life and items about sounds in different groups in each detail list.

The final step is to plan the organizational structure. There are two main organizational patterns:

1. An explanation of all the features of the first thing being compared; then an explanation of the second thing being compared. For example, you could write a complete discussion of life in the city followed by an explanation of life in the country.

2. Discussion of the first feature of the first thing being compared with the first feature of the second thing being compared; then the second feature, and so on. For example, one paragraph might concentrate on city and country sounds. The next paragraph might discuss social life in the city compared with social life in the country. Other paragraphs would each discuss separate features.

Both these organizational patterns need introductory and concluding material to help the reader understand your plan. As you do the following exercises, spend time planning the structure of your composition. Whichever plan you use, move from the least important to the most important details.

Exercises for Writing

1. Compare and contrast the person and the sculpture in the picture on page 71. First, list all the likenesses, and then list the differences. Write a short composition about this scene, using comparison and contrast to interest the reader.

2. Study the pictures on pages 72 and 73. List all the similarities between the two pictures you can find. Once you have done this, list all the differences you can find. Then write a composition in which you first discuss all of the similarities, then all of the differences.

3. Compare and contrast the two soldiers on pages 74 and 75. List all the similarities you can find. Then list all the differences. Write a composition comparing and contrasting the two people. In this composition, for each subtopic, first state the similarities, then the differences. For example, point out that both are carrying ammunition, then discuss the differences in what they are carrying, how they are carrying it, and so on.

4. Compare and contrast the woman and the painting on pages 76 and 77. These are two visuals of the same person. List the similarities then the differences. Use comparison and contrast to describe this person as the photographer and the artist tried to present her. Is this the same person to the photographer that she is to the artist?

72

On Your Own

1. In the following two paragraphs from an article in *Mademoiselle* magazine, Joyce Maynard explains the contrast between being 18 and 22.

> Well, I turned twenty-two a few months back, and an odd thing happened. I'd been prepared for the idea that someday I would probably be sixty-nine, and terrified of turning seventy, or thirty-nine, and depressed by forty, or even mildly saddened at the point when I turned thirty. I hadn't expected to feel sadness on my twenty-second birthday, and I did.
>
> It's not that I still wanted to be thought of as a kid; I think I like the bit of rounding out my body's gone through, since it was a boyish-looking seventeen. I don't miss my teenage voice, or my adolescent tendency to cuteness. I would rather be womanly. And I certainly didn't—don't—regard the age of twenty-two as over the hill, past the prime. What is past, though, is the very first bloom of youth. There is something in the face of an eighteen-year-old that's not in that same face four years later. The complexion may be clearer and the cheekbones more well-defined—the twenty-two-year-old face may be better-looking than the eighteen-year-old face ever was, but it was the eighteen-year-old who got smiled at, walking down the street, simply for being young.

Write a composition (at least two paragraphs) comparing yourself as you are today with how you were five or ten years ago.

2. Compare and contrast one or more of the following pairs. Create detail lists before you write.

- father and mother
- two sisters (or brothers)
- baby and adult

3. Compare and contrast one of your male friends with one of your female friends. Use detail lists first.

4. Compare and contrast one or more of the following:

- a dog and a cat
- a snake and a worm
- a rat and a squirrel
- a crow and a horse

5. Compare and contrast a place you love with a place you hate. List details first.

6. Compare and contrast two persons you like. List details.

7. Study the sky at night and list all the details you can. Then study the sky in the afternoon and list details. Compare and contrast these observations, using all the sensory details you can.

Summary

Comparison and contrast are at the heart of learning and critical thinking. The skills of detecting likenesses and differences lead us to judgments and opinions. Learn to perceive experiences and observations in terms of comparison and contrasts and use these skills when writing.

An unlearned carpenter of my acquaintance once said in my hearing, "There is very little difference between one man and another, but what little there is, is very important." This distinction seems to me to go to the root of the matter.

—William James

Simile and Metaphor

9

There are two useful techniques of comparison that effective writers learn to use well. Both are figures of speech. A *simile* generally states that something is like something else. On a hot day, you might say, "I feel like a doughnut in a baker's oven." The dancer might dance like a "live scarecrow on a sizzling frying pan." Such similes create colorful word-pictures that add zest to your writing.

A *metaphor* also sees one thing in terms of another. It pretends that something *is* something else. When Vachel Lindsay once wrote: "The moon is a silver cookie," we know it is not a cookie; he is merely seeing the moon in a fresh way.

Both metaphors and similes should be fresh. Stale metaphors and similes are clichés. Here are some examples of worn-out figures of speech:

- Busy as a bee
- Dull as ditchwater
- Thin as a rail

- She's an angel
- He is a prince
- White as a sheet

There are thousands of metaphor clichés and simile clichés. All of them are traps for the writer. It is dangerously easy to fall into the subtle snare of the cliché. When you do, you weaken your writing.

When you express yourself through a metaphor or simile, you should write with force and flashing lights. Striking comparisons electrify an idea, influence action, sharpen relationships, and intensify clarity.

Shakespeare was an ingenious master of the use of figures of speech. Where many would write "sleep well," he wrote ". . .enjoy the honey-heavy dew of slumber." He described nasty words as "poison more deadly than a mad dog's tooth."

Another writer, James Thurber, had very poor eyesight. Here is his description of an experience in botany:

> The instructor said I was supposed to look through the microscope and see a vivid, restless clockwork of sharply defined plant cells. "I see what looks like a lot of milk," I said.

Notice how effectively Annie Dillard describes a frog through similes:

At last I knelt . . . lost, dumbstruck, staring at the frog in the creek just four feet away. He was a very small frog with wide, dull eyes. And just as I looked at him, he slowly crumpled and began to sag. The spirit vanished from his eyes. His skin emptied and drooped; his very skull seemed to collapse like a kicked tent. He was shrinking before my eyes like a deflated football . . . Soon, part of his skin, formless as a pricked balloon, lay in floating folds like bright scum on top of the water.

Here are examples of the fresh use of simile and metaphor:

Violence in the city is <u>color blind</u>. It is an equal opportunity <u>disease</u> that has <u>infected</u> too many neighborhoods.
—Mike Barnicle, *The Boston Globe*

"WHAT!" yelled my schoolmaster, an Irishman with eyes <u>like broken glass</u>, and a <u>sniff of irritability</u> in the bristles of his nose.

—V.S. Pritchett

My mouth tastes <u>like the inside of a horse blanket</u>.
—Local slang

Merry <u>as a cricket</u>
—John Heywood, 16th century

A house is a <u>machine to live in</u>.
—Le Corbusier

As free <u>as a balloon cut from a string</u>.
—Anonymous

The red sun was pasted in the sky <u>like a fierce wafer</u>.
—Stephen Crane, *The Red Badge of Courage*

The shadows hung from the oak trees to the road <u>like curtains</u>.
—Eudora Welty, "The Worn Path."

Phrases of music seesawing crazily. Notes she had been practicing falling over each other <u>like a handful of marbles dropped downstairs</u>.
—Carson McCullers, "Wunderkind."

Exercises for Writing

1. For each of the pictures on pages 84 and 85 write a sentence using a simile or metaphor describing the situation pictured.

2. Use similes and metaphors in a composition to describe the musicians, the clothes, and the sounds going on in the picture on page 85.

3. Using similes or metaphors to describe what is happening, write a composition about the picture on page 86.

4. Study the picture on page 87. Complete the following with fresh similes:

    The eyebrows are like . . .

    The eyes are like . . .

    The nose is like . . .

    The lips are like . . .

    The ears are like . . .

    The complexion is like . . .

    The whole face is like . . .

When you have completed the sentences, write a composition about this picture. Use your similes in your composition.

84

Analogy

In Section 7, you were asked to explain similarities revealed directly in pairs of pictures. In this part of Section 9, you will be asked to explain an *analogy,* which is a comparison of two ideas that is hinted at in a single image or idea. An analogy might be visual or verbal. For example, Plato's famous analogy of the cave is explained in a lengthy composition.

He imagined men chained in a cave so that they could only look at one wall. Behind them, there was an opening in the cave through which light from the outside world reflected on the wall. On it, the prisoners could see shadows of people moving, and since they knew nothing about these actual people, they assumed the shadows were reality.

One day, the prisoners were released; when they saw actual people, they did not understand them or believe in them. They continued to think the shadows were real.

This contradiction, said Plato, is exactly like the refusal of ignorant, uneducated people — who have been brought up to believe in lies, illusions, and propaganda — to accept truth when it is revealed to them.

Plato's essay is full of reasoning, evidence, and proof of the analogy. An analogy is richer, deeper, and more complex than a simile or metaphor but is based on the same mental process: observing or imagining a likeness.

Here are two examples of analogies, one by a professional writer, and one by a student. Study them carefully as models for what you will be asked to write about after you study the pictures. Ask yourself whether the similarities are phony, mysterious, harsh, superficial, amusing, accurate, forced, and/or convincing.

> Trees, trees, millions of trees, massive, immense, running
> up high; and at their foot, hugging the bank against the
> stream, crept the little begrimed steamer, like a sluggish
> beetle crawling on the floor of a lofty portico. It made you
> feel very small, very lost, and yet it was not altogether
> depressing, that feeling. After all, if you were small, the
> grimy beetle crawled on—which was just what you
> wanted it to do . . . when the steam pipes started leaking
> we crawled very slow. The reaches opened before us and

closed behind, as if the forest had stepped leisurely across the water to bar the way for our return. We penetrated deeper and deeper into the heart of darkness. It was very quiet there.

—from *Heart of Darkness,* by Joseph Conrad

Friendships are like beautiful china dolls. They are painstakingly formed, yet so easily broken if not handled with care. Both will usually last forever unless they are abused. Once the china doll becomes broken, it remains shattered in a million tiny pieces. It may be replaced by another doll which may be just as good and resembles it closely, but it will not be exactly the same. Sometimes it is possible to glue the doll back together if the damage is not too severe, but the cracks or "scars" will always be visible, constant reminders of the damage done. This is true with friendships. Once broken, they will never be exactly the same as before, even if they do get "glued" back together. If one carefully handles a friendship, it will stay beautiful for a very long time, just like the china doll that has been cared for. Friendships, like the dolls, if not broken, may become faded and temporarily forgotten on the back of a shelf or in the recesses of one's mind. But, having a faded, forgotten, old china doll with happy memories attached is much better than never having one at all.

—from a student essay

Exercises for writing

1. Study all of the following pictures. Select the one that interests you most and write an analogy in at least one paragraph. Follow the pattern of one of the analogies you have just read.

2. Examine the picture on page 96. Give it a metaphorical title that will reflect the mood and the combination of images in it. Write a composition based upon the picture as a metaphor, using metaphors and similes based upon specific images in the picture.

"Don't be afraid, dear—it's a tree!"

On Your Own

1. Write three similes to describe three physical characteristics of a person you know. Some physical characteristics are hairstyle, smile, walk, nervous habit.

2. Write metaphors to describe the following:

- a pet — how it sounds, shows affection, looks
- a car — how it moves, how the engine sounds
- a vegetable — one you hate to eat
- a person — the personality traits of someone you like

3. Find an interesting place and people to observe. Describe the people and objects with similes and metaphors.

4. Write a composition using an analogy to describe one of the following:

- a school
- a frightening experience
- an incident that made you laugh
- a person you admire

Summary

Good writers have always used similes, metaphors, and analogies to create striking word-pictures for readers. The skillful use of these figures of speech can help you to write prose and poetry that will have power and punch.

> *The metaphor is probably the most fertile*
> *power possessed by man.*
> —Jose Ortega Y Gasset

> *One simile that solitary shines*
> *In the dry desert of a thousand lines.*
> —Alexander Pope

Emphasizing Ideas 10

One of the most difficult and important aspects of writing is emphasis, which means saying something so that it stands out — like a lighted match on a blacked-out stage. If your composition is weak, one reason may be that your good ideas have been poorly, vaguely, or wrongly emphasized, so that they do not appear to be more important than others.

In writing, strong emphasis depends on two general principles: the position of words and ideas, and the choice of material to develop your purpose. Following are techniques used by good writers to make vital points outstanding.

1. Place the most important material at the end, in sentences, in paragraphs, and in the whole essay.

2. Use concrete words rather than general abstract terms.

3. Use comparisons. Saying what something is like is often stronger than merely naming it.

4. Sometimes, a contrast is forceful. An expression, an object, an action, a relationship, may be sharply defined by saying what it is NOT. For example:

She looks lonely, and I don't mean all alone, because I don't think she seems to be wishing her boyfriend would appear. I think she's lonely for something to do besides reading that dull book.
   —from an essay about the picture on page 105.

Jazz music is different than rock music. That doesn't mean it's better, though I personally like it better. It means that the purposes are not the same: jazz tries to invent; rock tries to repeat.
   —student essay

5. Use common words in uncommon combinations. For example, surprise the reader by altering a cliché:

She stood there looking at him, calm and disconnected.

As you can see, emphasis depends a great deal on organization and the choice of ideas. Once you have chosen an idea and an attitude for a composition, a profitable next step can be to make a sentence list to help you organize your ideas. You will need to choose main ideas and the sub-points for the main ideas.

In a well organized essay, the second paragraph logically follows the first, the third develops out of the second, and so on to the conclusion. When you can see this organization at a glance, you can make sure each paragraph advances and expands — NOT just repeats — your main point. This device will help you to produce tight and clear connections between paragraphs, and it will help you emphasize your ideas.

In making such a list, write out one complete sentence for each paragraph — not just a word or phrase. If you find that some connections are not clear when you read through your list, you will be able to tell where you simply are repeating, where you have wandered, and when a paragraph is out of place.

Exercises for Writing

1. Study the picture on page 103. What is the emphasis in this picture? Write a composition that illustrates and emphasizes the main point of the picture. Begin your planning with a sentence list.

2. Write a paragraph explaining the mood of the picture on page 104. Use some of the special devices to give emphasis.

3. Write a paragraph describing the picture on page 106. Decide what to emphasize in writing about this picture. Use some devices to give emphasis.

4. Describe the picture on page 108 using a metaphor or simile to emphasize the main point. Support your idea with details.

5. Study the following student composition written about the photograph on page 108. Pay particular attention to the placement of ideas and images in relation to the main point. Notice how the writer used details and position to give emphasis. Are there additional places where these techniques could have been used?

The Sand

Billions of them are heaped up in great, white, dry mounds. They are jammed together, successively more compressed by others like them, until at the bottom of the mound the pressures exerted by each can only be measured in thousands of pounds per square inch. Still they are not crushed. Each particle of sand remains whole and intact, as if it were indivisible.

Those near the surface are whipped into space by pretentious blasts of wind and are carried for miles, constantly colliding with one another at frenzied velocities. They rebound erratically, crashing through the sea of mayhem that surrounds them, which is themselves. But they are not broken.

Finally they come to rest again heaped one upon another. They are intimate, especially those deeply buried, but they don't recognize one another. For they are all the same, and always have been, and always will be.

A plane falls, a thirsty man crawls, a wind blows, and they are in the air. They bury the plane and stifle the man, but they are not moved except by the merciless currents that jostle them aloft. The plane and the man are gone, and only a few of them know to where. But they will never tell, for they are like the others. They will continue to mutely shift, slide, and collide as they always have and always will.

6. Read the following excerpt from Stephen Crane's story, "The Blue Hotel." What main point is emphasized in this excerpt? What images provide support and background for the main point? Write the answers to these questions.

The Swede backed rapidly toward the corner of the room. His hands were out protectingly in front of his chest, but he was making an obvious struggle to control his fright.

"Gentlemen," he quavered, "I suppose I am going to be killed before I can leave this house! I suppose I am going to be killed before I can leave this house!" In his eyes was a dying swan look. Through the windows could be seen the snow turning blue in the shadow of dusk. The wind tore at the house, and some loose thing beat regularly against the clapboards like a spirit tapping.

—Stephen Crane, "The Blue Hotel"

7. In the following two paragraphs, which open John D. MacDonald's suspense novel *One Fearful Yellow Eye,* certain very definite feelings about air travel are emphasized. What are they, and how does the writer create them?

Around and around we went, like circling through wads of lint in a dirty pocket. We'd been in that high blue up yonder where it was a bright cold clear December afternoon, and then we had to go down into that guck, as it was the intention of the airline and the airplane driver to put the 727 down at O'Hare.

Passengers reached up and put their lights on. The sky had lumps and holes in it. It becomes tight-sphincter time in the sky when they don't insert the ship into the pattern and get it down, but go around again. Stewardesses walk tippy-dainty, their color not good in the inside lights, their smiles sutured so firmly in place it pulls their pretty faces more distinctly against the skull-shape of pretty bones. Even with the buffeting, there is an impression of silence inside the aircraft at such times. People stare outward, but they are looking inward, tasting of themselves and thinking of promises and defeats. The busy air is full of premonitions, and one thinks with a certain comfort of old Satchel's plug in favor of air travel: "They may kill you, but they ain't likely to hurt you."

On Your Own

1. Write a composition that describes a friend. Before you begin, decide the main point that you want to emphasize about this person. What details (actions, qualities, talents) contribute to this main point? Plan your composition using a sentence list.

2. Select a movie you have recently seen. What is the main point of the movie? What scenes contributed most to this point? Write a composition emphasizing the main point through details. Do not simply retell the story.

3. Study a painting in an art gallery or book. What does the artist emphasize in the painting? How? Write a composition explaining how the main idea or mood is emphasized.

Summary

Any good writer knows that some points are more important than others and that the main points must hit the reader so they will be remembered. The major figures are clearly emphasized against a ground of supporting points and details. Know the major points and state them well, against a background of explanation and support.

> *The problem is to teach ourselves to think,*
> *and the writing will take care of itself.*
> —Christopher Morley

Point of View
11

Point of view has several basic meanings in the writing process. The first is concerned with how a story is told. First person point of view uses *I* or *we* to relate the action. If a story begins, "I awoke and heard a loud explosion," the point of view is the first person.

Third person point of view uses *he, she, it, they* or the characters' names to relate the action, as in the following:

- He awoke and heard a loud explosion.
- Gloria awoke and heard a loud explosion.
- The rabbit awoke when it heard a loud explosion.
- They awoke when they heard a loud explosion.

The third person point of view can be either *omniscient* (meaning all-knowing) or *objective.* The omniscient story teller knows what all the characters think and feel and what happens in the story. The omniscient writer may also give opinions about the events and interpret the actions for the reader. The objective story-teller merely tells the story and lets the reader form opinions.

Another meaning of point of view involves feelings or beliefs. The attitudes, ideas, and feelings of the writer or a character toward a situation depend upon experience, habits, social position, and many other elements in the background of the person. From a starving person's point of view, a candy bar may be a life-saver, whereas a health food enthusiast may view it as junk food not worth eating.

The physical position from which you experience an event is also part of point of view. If you sit in the front row at a concert, you can see as well as hear the performers. If you are so far away from the stage that you can hardly see the performers, the concert is an entirely different experience. If you saw an accident from a window 20 stories high, it would be a different experience from seeing the accident 20 feet away on the street.

As you can see, the selection of a point of view affects every aspect of writing. Before starting to write, consider whether you will use first, second, or third person. Also, determine your attitude toward your subject. Do you strongly like or dislike the person or event or idea you are writing about? Are you physically close, distant, above, below, your subject? How does your position affect what you have to say?

Exercises for Writing

1. Study the two pictures on pages 114 and 115. Write a composition that compares and contrasts the bird soaring over the fields or over the city with a man or woman who views the bird soaring overhead. What does the soaring bird see? What does the man or woman see?

2. Study the picture on 116. Describe how the person looks in this picture and then imagine how the person would look if you met him or her face to face.

3. Describe the football player as he appears in the picture on page 117. Compare and contrast that image with how he might look from the top row of a stadium.

4. Study the picture on page 118. There is a dramatic situation here. First, decide what the main point of the situation is. Then, list the details and feelings from the various points of view of the people. After you have listed these, write a composition about the situation that includes:

    a. the point of view of the waiter

    b. the point of view of the man in the foreground talking to the waiter

    c. the point of view of the girl in the center with her hand on her chin

    d. the point of view of the man drinking from a glass

    e. the point of view of the girl with the back of her head to the camera

5. Sometimes a photographer, painter, or sculptor may reveal personal attitudes in a visual work of art. Look through this book and find a picture you feel is trying to convey a personal point to the viewer — to influence the viewer to think a certain way. Whether you agree or disagree with the artist, write a composition that expresses the point of view. Support what you say with evidence and details.

6. In John Godfrey Saxe's "The Blind Men and the Elephant," six blind men go to "see" an elephant so "each by observation might satisfy his mind." The following are each man's observation of the elephant.

    a. "God bless me but the Elephant is very like a wall!"

    b. "This wonder of an Elephant is very like a spear!"

    c. "I see the elephant is very like a snake!"

    d. "Tis clear enough the Elephant is very like a tree!"

    e. "This marvel of an Elephant is very like a fan!"

    f. "I see," quoth he, "the elephant is very like a rope!"

Each blind man, through the sense of touch, has formed a unique point of view about the elephant. Write a composition that explains how each man reached his conclusion, and why each was "partly right" but all were wrong. What is the main idea that the story poem is trying to illustrate?

7. Write a composition about the quotation below that will answer the question that Victor Hugo poses. What does the quotation imply about point of view?

> *Where the telescope ends, the microscope begins.*
> *Which of the two has the grander view?*
>   —Victor Hugo

On Your Own

1. Think of an argument you have had with a friend or a relative. Write a composition that states clearly the point of view of the person you opposed. Then write your own point of view. Draw a reasonable and fair conclusion from the two viewpoints.

2. If possible, listen to two sides of a political issue. Write a composition that states both viewpoints. Draw a conclusion that is based upon the facts and is reasonable.

3. Find an editorial in a newspaper on a subject that interests you. Write an editorial that opposes the newspaper's viewpoint.

4. Select one of the following stories and retell it from the point of view of the character.

> a. Jack and the Beanstalk from the point of view of the giant
>
> b. Little Red Riding Hood from the point of view of the wolf
>
> c. Cinderella from the point of view of one of the ugly sisters

5. Select a novel or short story that interests you. Explain the author's point of view and point out how it affects the emphasis of the writing and the development of the story. How effective would the story be if it were written from a different point of view?

Summary

Whenever you write, you must decide what audience you are trying to reach. Once you assess your audience, you must develop your writing from a point of view that includes your attitudes and feelings about the subject. Familiarize yourself with the advantages and disadvantages of using first person, third person, and omniscient types of development. What you write depends on how you view what you wish to say.

> *I write from the worm's eye point of view.*
> —Ernie Pyle

Seeing an Idea

12

A ny good essay is based upon an idea. An idea is a thought, a conception, an opinion, a conviction, or a principle. Ideas are abstract until they are made clear by illustrations or examples. The task of the writer is to take the germ of an idea and make it grow into clarity through concrete development.

Labels may stimulate ideas, but they do not stand up as clear ideas because they have different meanings for different people. *Liberty, love,* and *religion* are abstract labels that have meaning for a person only through the sum of experience and background.

Suppose you were asked to write an essay on *athletics.* This subject is so broad that it could be treated in many different ways. You could describe all the sports you know. You could argue that athletic competition builds character. You could also write a negative piece from the point of view that sports competition injures and even kills many people each year.

You, the writer, have to decide what you want to express about a topic and limit it clearly so you can handle it. You should be able to express your main idea in one sentence (the thesis sentence) and develop it within the limits of that sentence.

If you think that athletic competition builds character, you begin with a thesis sentence.

> I think participation in athletic competition builds character.

This sentence, or one similar to it, should appear early in your composition to make your viewpoint and the limits of the essay clear to the reader. The rest of the composition should show the reader through evidence, illustrations, and examples why you feel this way about athletics.

In the following short compositions about the picture on page 126, each writer states a general idea about flies and then develops it emphatically with evidence. Each one, furthermore, states the main idea as a complete thought in a complete sentence, as underlined.

> The fly was drunk with sunshine. From time to time its wings would quiver with brief frenzy. When the joy and intermingled pain of the smoldering cobblestones beneath its feet became too intense, it would lift them one by one. The brightness of the pavement sifted through its

many-faceted eyes and splashed warm red throughout its skull. Its antennae were relaxed from nervous vigil and calmly nodded in the air currents rising from the stones. It had no reason to be wary; no, not on the pavement of the wide courtyard deserted by almost all for the cool shade of porches. Thus it rested in safety in the middle of a vast, empty field of heat.

— from a student essay

I believe we can nowhere find a better type of perfectly free creature than in the common house fly.
Not free only but brave; and irreverent to a degree which I think no human republican could by any philosophy exalt himself to; he has no work to do, no tyrannical instinct to obey. The earthworm has his digging; the bee her gathering and building; the spider his cunning network; the ant her treasury and accounts. All these are slaves, or people of vulgar business. But your fly, free in the air, free in the chamber—a black incarnation of caprice wandering, investigating, flitting, flirting, feasting at his will, with rich variety of choice, from the heaped sweets in the grocer's window to those of the butcher's backyard, and from the galled places on a horse's back to the brown spot in the road from which, as the foot disturbs him, he rises with angry republican buzz.
What freedom is like his?

—John Ruskin

The ordinary house fly can be one of the most dangerous insects you can encounter. This uninvited guest may spoil much more than your picnic. By transmitting germs, house flies can cause serious illness and even death. Flies have a sticky substance on their feet that enables them to walk upside down on the ceiling or up a wall. This substance will pick up germs and later deposit the bacteria elsewhere. If humans contact and assimilate the wrong bacteria at the wrong time, the consequences can be serious or even lethal. House flies can carry over thirty diseases that include scarlet fever, typhoid fever, spinal meningitis, dysentery, and smallpox. It is wise to view the house fly as an enemy and to destroy it on sight. Remember the proverb: "Even a lion must fight flies."

—David A. Sohn

122

Exercises for Writing

1. Study the picture on page 124. State in one sentence a major idea that this picture suggests to you. Then list details that will illustrate and support your idea. Begin by writing, "This picture shows that . . ." Once you have stated the idea, cross out "This picture shows that" and you will have your idea. The rest of your composition should explain to the reader, through details and illustrations, why and how the statement is true.

2. Write two possible thesis statements for the picture on page 125. Develop one idea through details based upon the picture and your experience.

3. What idea does the picture on page 126 suggest to you? State your idea in one sentence then write a composition developing your idea.

4. What major idea does the picture on page 127 suggest to you? State it in one sentence and write a composition showing why your idea is reasonable and believable.

124

On Your Own

1. Observe a crowd or a group in action: at a meeting, athletic event, restaurant, rehearsal, or any situation you can observe. Sit still and listen. Observe gestures, facial expressions, physical relationships, and attitudes. Listen to words and sounds. What is going on under the surface? Is there a conflict? What do you notice about the people?

Afterwards, try to abstract from all the details a general meaning or idea about the way those people were behaving, like this for example:

> It was a quiet group, as if waiting for someone to stir them up.

> Nobody was listening to anybody else. They were all isolated inside, each one trying to sound off with his own ideas. It was chaotic.

Write a fully developed paragraph explaining your conclusion about what was going on. Use as many details as possible from the scene and express the whole paragraph as if you were trying to communicate to someone who wasn't there. Now do the same thing but do not state the general idea directly. Choose specific details to show your reader your conclusion.

2. Listen to a speech in person or on radio or television. What is the main idea of the speech? List illustrations or examples that the speaker uses to support the idea.

3. Listen to the lyrics of three popular songs. What are the main ideas of these songs? Does each song illustrate the main idea sufficiently to convince the listener? Write a composition explaining how the writers used emphasis to make their points.

4. Select a movie that interests you. What is the main idea of the movie? What scenes or sequences support the main idea? Was the movie convincing? In a brief essay discuss why or why not.

5. Select a short story that interests you. What is the main idea of the story? In a short composition explain how the writer emphasizes that idea.

6. Study three commercials on television. What visuals and words are used to convince the viewer to buy the products? Are the commercials convincing? Do the commercials leave out any important information that might cause the viewer to reject the product? Write one paragraph per commercial explaining how the main point is given emphasis.

Summary

When a writer has something important to express, the idea must be clarified so that the reader will understand it. Further explanation through examples, illustrations, and supporting details should reinforce the idea clearly. Alfred North Whitehead's statement, "We think in generalities. We live in detail" can be related to writing. Generalities (ideas) must use the world of detail to achieve a clear effect for the reader.

> *An idea is a feat of association.*
> —Robert Frost

> *Time was invented by Almighty God in order to give ideas a chance.*
> —Nicholas Murray Butler

Using
Humor
13

Humor depends upon surprise, an element of the unexpected that causes a smile or a roar of laughter. We laugh when a person gets a pie in the face because it is an unexpected action that jolts the composure of the victim.

Humor can also be cruel. A philosopher once said that people laugh because they feel superior. Sarcasm is always an attempt to belittle someone else through a cutting remark. Ethnic jokes are generally attempts to achieve humor by making a race, group, or nationality appear stupid and the teller of the joke appear superior.

Visual humor includes some element of visual surprise. Verbal humor depends on surprise through language. Humor is effective when the surprise is fresh and clever. It fails when the attempt at humor is predictable or when it hurts the audience through bad taste. The punch line of a good joke must have a fresh punch to evoke laughter.

The pictures in this section were included partly for the fun of it and partly for variety. In addition, they are intended to suggest the use of humor as a way of developing an idea.

Exercises for Writing

1. In a way, a genuinely humorous photograph is like a good one-liner. Write one-liners for four of the pictures in this section.

2. Write a simile or metaphor that fits the mood of one particular picture.

3. Write a brief monologue for one of the animal pictures.

4. What is unexpected about the picture on page 135? Write a humorous story from the point of view of the character in the picture.

5. Study the picture on page 136. Compare and contrast in a humorous way this picture with Leonardo da Vinci's *Mona Lisa*.

6. Write a humorous composition about the picture on page 137 explaining how this statue lost its head and how it feels about it.

132

On Your Own

1. Write a joke you think is funny. Explain what makes it funny.

2. Cut out two comic strips from magazines. Explain why they are funny.

3. Write a composition about a humorous experience you have had.

4. Select a comedian from television who you feel is effective. Write a composition explaining how and why you think the comedian is funny.

5. What is the funniest movie you have seen? Write a composition explaining why it was funny.

6. Describe a scene in which some observers laughed and others didn't. Explain the reasons for the different reactions.

Summary

Humor takes many forms. In writing, humor may be broad or subtle, clever or obvious. The writer must be careful with humor, remembering that the most effective humor is neither offensive nor cruel.

Often humor depends upon comparison and timing. When Mark Twain said, "Thunder is good, thunder is impressive, but it is lightning that does the work," he wrote a clever metaphor for human behavior. It was a clever way of saying, "Deeds are more important than words" or "Talk is cheap." For any writer, humor is a fine tool if the writer uses it carefully and well.

> *All the fun's in how you say a thing.*
> —Robert Frost

Describing Conflict

14

GET MEN BACK TO WORK!

The subject matter of most good writing includes conflict and opposition. Any student who says, hopelessly, "but I don't know what to write about," should start looking for adversaries, opponents, contrasts, contests. If you feel like writing about Friendship or My Philosophy or Families, don't stop with such general labels; think of conflicts in these areas, and you are on the way to good subject material.

The pictures in this section were chosen to dramatize conflict as interesting and important subject matter in both photography and writing. In each image, there is something worth writing about because of the strong emotions revealed.

Some of the scenes highlight physical opposition. Others show tension that is not obvious in motion and action. The torment is internal, suggested by small details, such as contrasts in lines, ideas, forces, shapes, or a look.

Most of the conflicts are complicated. That is, the pictures raise questions that you need to answer before you write a composition. Before putting words on paper, analyze each picture to find out how much material it suggests. See if you can find enough for a composition of several paragraphs.

Here is a list of some parts of an image that might be turned into separate paragraphs:

- details of physical conflict
- details suggesting inner turmoil
- causes and effects
- mood of the conflict: harsh, subdued, mysterious
- your personal reaction: Do you favor one side?
- possible thoughts of the characters
- possible resolution to the struggle

Exercises for Writing

1. What is the conflict in the picture on page 143? List the details that illustrate this conflict. Write a composition that describes the conflict and how it is resolved.

2. Study the picture on page 144. Describe the picture in detail and show how the picture is a symbol of conflict between two nations or groups.

3. What is the situation pictured on page 145? Write a composition which states the problem and conflict and describes how it might be resolved.

4. Describe the picture on page 146 in detail. What is causing the conflict? Write a composition that describes the conflict and suggests a possible resolution.

5. Decide what is causing the conflict within the main character in the picture on page 147. Write a first-person composition in which the character states the problem and a solution.

6. Study the scene pictured on page 148. What is the problem? The conflict? Write a composition showing how the situation ends.

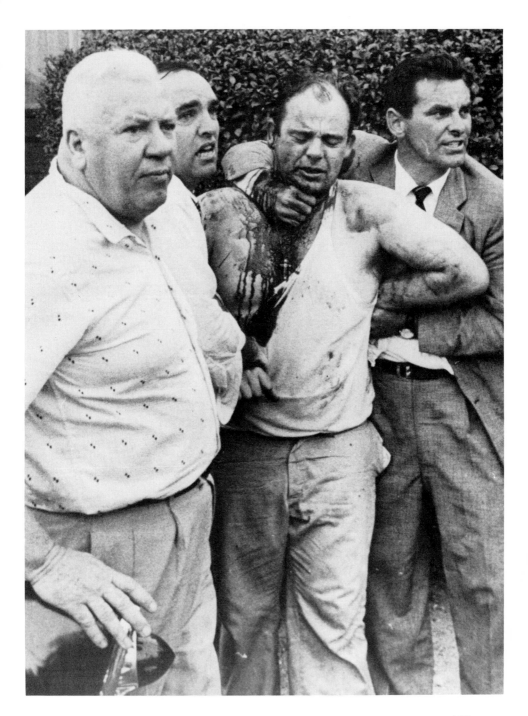

On Your Own

1. Write a dialogue between two people who disagree about what to have for dinner. The argument may lead to a larger conflict if you wish.

2. Use the following first lines to create a problem and a conflict for the characters:

> Bill and Mary awoke on a beautiful day filled with sunshine. Then, everything collapsed!

Write a composition describing the problem, explaining its causes and probable effects on Bill's and Mary's lives.

3. Write an essay describing the thoughts of a person who feels a friend has stolen something valuable from him or her.

4. Think of a major conflict you have experienced in the past. Write a composition describing how the problem was solved or not solved.

5. One writing technique often used by writers is to begin an essay with a brief story that illustrates a point to be further developed in the essay. Try using this technique. For any of the pictures in this section, plan an essay on the central conflict, then write the essay, beginning with a story.

Summary

Without problems and conflicts there would be no dramatic interest in stories, novels, plays, and movies. Would a description of your typical day be of much interest to anybody but you? Remember that the art of story telling depends on interesting characters facing interesting problems. With practice, you can use conflict as a device to tell a story well.

> *Everything written is as good*
> *as it is dramatic.*
> —Robert Frost

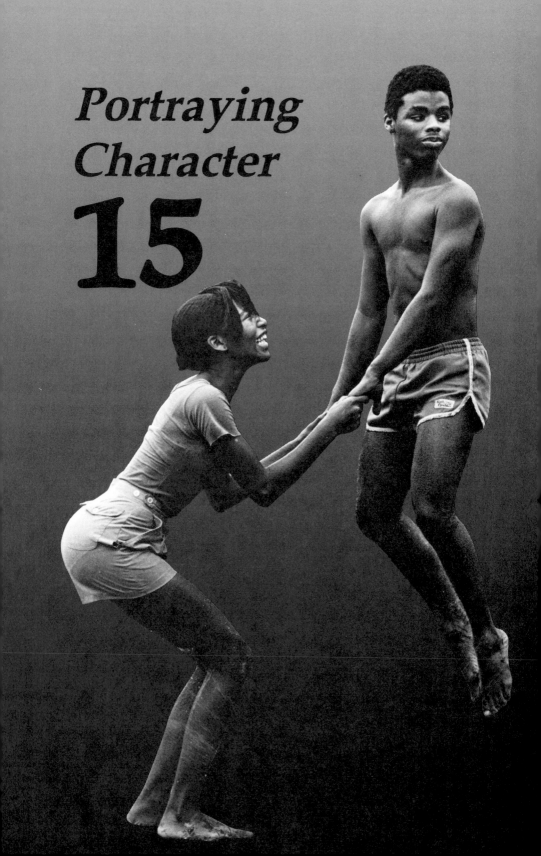

*Portraying
Character*
15

One of the most powerful forces in human life is character. It is so strong that thousands of writers throughout literary history have placed more emphasis on character than any other element. You probably have been made aware of this in your study of stories, novels, and plays. You may have been asked to consider the nature of this character, the thoughts of that one, the motives of another, and the way one individual is related to another.

The importance of character and personality is so great that in the settling of human conflict, one of the first things analyzed is not just *what* was done but *why*. This involves the hard task of figuring out what goes on in the mind and heart of a person.

There are various ways of discovering such truths, but one of the most important is the study of facial expressions, gestures, tones of voice, and movements of the body. These are the outward signs of thought and feeling, and although they may be misleading, they are so often right that they cannot be ignored. In the best sense of the word, you are only partly educated until you have learned by reading such signs, to observe some of the truths of character.

The pictures in this section have been selected because they reveal character through expression, gesture, and action. Look carefully at the curve of a mouth, the flick of an eye, the posture of the whole body. What do all these details suggest about the individual? What traits would you expect to find in each person? What would you expect the person to do in an argument or fight?

As you do the exercises in this section, pay special attention to finding the most exact and suggestive words for what you see. Think of similes and metaphors to describe a face, a gesture, an action.

There are many ways to write about character. One is to make a direct statement: "She is shy." or "He is proud." The next step is to *show* how these traits appear in the actions or words of the person.

Another way to write about character is not to make direct statements but to describe individual reactions so clearly that the reader understands the aspects of character that are revealed.

A third approach is to imagine what the person is thinking and then write out the thoughts so realistically that the reader will recognize motives and attitudes. A variation of this is to write a dialogue that suggests the nature of the person.

Here are brief examples of clear insight into the meaning of character as revealed by visual evidence:

> Yon Cassius hath a lean and hungry look,
> He likes not music.
> Let me have men about me that are fat.
> —from *Julius Caesar* by Shakespeare

> He never learned a trade, he just sells gas, checks oil, and changes flats. Once in a while, as a gag, he dribbles an inner tube.
> —from "Ex-basketball Player" by John Updike

> ...and for the past two years I had lived in intimacy with college students, the most open, the most threatened, most serious, most generous people I had ever known.
> —from *The Algiers Motel Incident* by John Hersey

Exercises for Writing

1. Study each of the pictures in this section. Write one sentence for each that sums up the character or characters as depicted in the situation.

2. Study the picture of General Eisenhower on page 154. Write a paragraph describing what you see of his character.

3. Write paragraphs about each character in the picture on page 155. Support your conclusions about each character with details from the picture.

4. What might one character in the picture on page 156 be saying? What might the other character be thinking? Write a paragraph using their words and thoughts to bring out their characters.

5. What might the character in the picture on page 157 be saying to herself? Mental conversation with oneself is called interior monologue. Write an interior monologue in which the character's thoughts reveal something about her character.

6. Study the picture on page 158. Write several sentences for each of the four men in the foreground which express their thoughts about the two women they are observing and also something about their own characters. Then write a dialogue between the two women which comments on the men observing them.

7. What might be the problem situation in the picture on page 159? Write out a conversation among these men that suggests the character of each man.

8. Write an interior monologue that expresses how one of the soldiers pictured on page 160 feels about the leader. Then write an interior monologue for the leader which shows how she feels about the men.

9. Write out the words of the coach pictured on page 161. Choose words that reveal his character.

10. Write an interior monologue for each of the two people in the picture on page 162. Show how they feel about each other and about themselves.

154

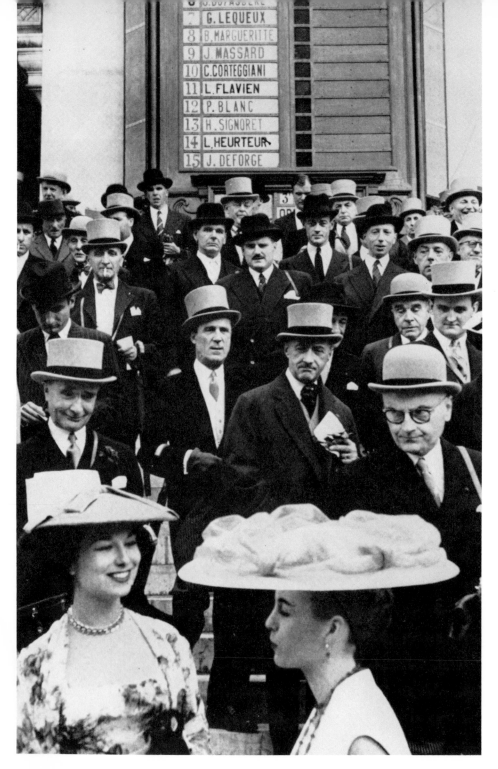

On Your Own

1. Write a detailed character sketch about someone you know. What does the person look like? How does the person act and think?

2. Select one of the most interesting characters from your reading of stories, novels, or plays. Write a composition explaining why this character is one of your favorites. Give specific examples to illustrate your points.

3. Select one of your favorite characters from a movie or a television show. Describe this character and explain why he or she is one of your favorite characters.

4. Write a character description of one of the people you have admired most in the past.

5. Write a character description of one of the people you have disliked most in the past.

Summary

Creating believable, well-defined characters is one of the most difficult tasks a writer faces. It is so easy to fall into the trap of creating a stock character who looks and sounds like thousands of other people. Such a character is called a stereotype, and a stereotype is equivalent to cliché writing. Writers of soap operas and situation comedies frequently use stereotypes for their characters.

The only way to learn to create original characters is to observe people as individuals and learn how they look, walk, think, and talk.

When writing a story, your creative imagination will help you to form believable characters based upon your observations of actual people and your inventive powers. Keen observation is the key to creating interesting characters.

> One's eyes are what one is,
> one's mouth what one becomes.
> —John Galsworthy

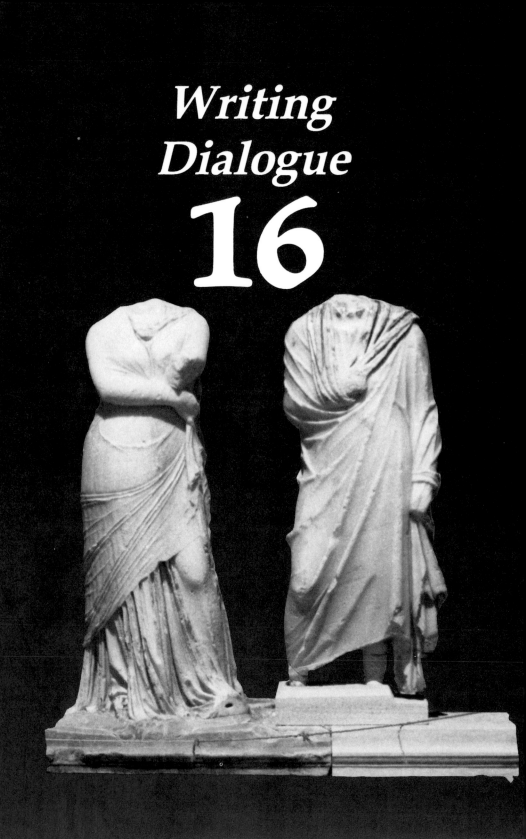

Writing Dialogue

16

In the previous section you explored character as revealed through pictures. You speculated about what the persons in the pictures were thinking, reflecting, feeling. Because what people think and feel is usually directly related to what they say, character is clearly shown in dialogue. In this chapter you will carry your interpretation of character one step further by speculating about what people are saying to each other.

Study the people in the following pictures and try to imagine what they were saying when the picture was taken. If you can't see enough solid evidence in the pictures, make up a background that would logically lead to what is shown. This might mean deciding that the characters were involved in some kind of conflict. That could tell you what they were saying and in what manner and what tone of voice.

The standard way of writing dialogue is to identify the speakers in a brief sentence or paragraph and then write what they say within quotation marks. Here is an example based on the picture on page 168.

Two students are having an argument.

She. "But that's not what I said."
He. "But that's what you MEANT."

Or you can use a form like this:

Eddie said accusingly, "You mean you don't want to go
out with me!"
Maria answered, "You catch on very quickly."

Conventional punctuation rules require that any form of *to say* is followed by a comma, then quotation marks. All quotations begin with a capital letter as in the examples above. If reference words break up a sentence, however, the second part begins with a lowercase letter.

"The trouble with you," the senator said, "is that you
can't make up your mind."

Commas go inside quotation marks; semicolons and colons always go outside the quotation marks. Question marks go inside or outside depending on whether they are part of the quoted passage.

> "Ready?" asked the referee.
> Why did he say, "You must pay a penalty"?

Finally, in writing dialogue, always begin a new paragraph with a change of speaker.

Exercises for Writing

1. For each of the pictures in this section imagine what has happened before the picture was taken and what happens afterwards. Then write a brief description of the situation followed by a dialogue between the people pictured. Pay attention to not only what they say, but *how*.

2. Write a dialogue between the two statues on page 167. Have them discuss the circumstances in which they lost their heads.

3. Write a brief dialogue among the three persons in the picture on page 169. Imagine what they were saying when the picture was taken and write it out.

4. Study the picture on page 171. Write dialogues between the man and the woman for each of the following situations:

    a. The man is trying to borrow money from the woman.

    b. The woman thinks that the man (her sweetheart) has been dating another woman.

    c. Someone is following them.

On Your Own

As you write the following dialogues, pay attention to *how* you want the character to speak. You may have to alter spelling to indicate, for instance, a British accent, street slang, a "formal" character.

1. Create an imaginary dialogue between yourself and one of the following about a problem situation:

> a parent
>
> a friend
>
> a person you dislike

2. From a distance, observe two people who are having a discussion. Watch their gestures, facial expressions, and other body language. Write out their conversation in the form of a dialogue.

3. After you have turned off the sound of a television set, observe one scene of a soap opera or other dramatic show. Write the dialogue as you imagine it.

4. Write a dialogue between yourself and a dead character from history who has returned to life. Explain the present world as you perceive it to the character and write his or her reactions.

5. Interview an animal. Imagine a conversation you might have with the animal if it could talk. You might include some unusual sounds in the animal's speech.

6. This is supposed to be one of the shortest stories ever written:

> He was the last man in the world. Suddenly there was a knock on the door.

Write a dialogue between the man and whatever was knocking.

Summary

Effective writers have good ears. They learn to listen to what people say and how they express themselves. They gain a feel for the rhythms and the sounds of language. When writing good dialogue, the words have to sound natural. The development of a dialogue should also progress naturally toward some dramatic point. Practice good listening and keep a notebook for unusual expressions or interesting snatches of dialogue. An excellent listener can develop an ear for spoken language and use it well in writing.

Speech is a mirror of the soul;
as a man speaks, so is he.
—Publius Syrus, Maxim 1073

It takes two to speak the truth—
one to speak and another to hear.
—Henry David Thoreau

I am not arguing with you—I am telling you.
—James McNeill Whistler

Stop; look; listen.
—Ralph R. Upton
Notice at American
Railroad Crossings, 1912

Creating
Narratives
17

When the basic idea of a composition is developed by telling a story, the type of development is called *narration*. Short stories, plays, novels, fables, parables, and even jokes are examples of this method of development.

Storytelling has been a favorite form of entertainment and enlightenment since cavemen and cavewomen sat around the fire. Any story ordinarily begins with a description of the place and time (setting), then an introduction of the characters and a problem they face. What happens as the characters attempt to solve the problem is called the plot.

The problem usually sets up a conflict which creates interest, builds the tension as the plot develops, reaches a crisis or turning point, and is resolved in a climax and final wrapping up of details.

Short narratives, often called anecdotes, can be used to dramatize ideas. Such anecdotes are useful in many types of writing. Here, you will be asked to write a longer narrative for its own sake based on six photographs of a cat-and-mouse drama that took place in the author's kitchen.

Your assignment is to write a full account of what happened by organizing the actual events shown, according to certain principles of narration:

1. Describe your characters (the cat and mouse) and give some indication of what they are like as animals. You may wish to give them names, as well, that indicate something about their characters.

2. First comes the process of selection. In almost any story there is more material than can be used in the time and space available. The photographer, for example, took 24 pictures but could only use six in this book. Each of the ones here was chosen because it emphasized an important part of the story. That is, it contributed a strong image. For this story the selections have been made for you.

3. The most common technique of storytelling follows a chronological order. Make sure that you express, or suggest, the logical and emotional connections, so that each happening is seen to result from the one before it.

   To make good connections you may have to use your imagination to create and interpret the facts, since an image may mean more than it actually shows. What, for example, is the point of the second picture? What may have happened between the last two pictures?

Sometimes a flashback may be useful to describe previous events that give additional meaning to the immediate action. For example, you might mention a time when the mouse got away.

4. Include description with your narrative to convey exactly what happened and to create the spirit of the important moments. Sharp physical words are vital, and the use of comparison and contrast can improve the narration.

5. Some writers openly state an idea such as, "The cat-and-mouse game is devious, cruel, and one-sided." The modern tendency, however, is to avoid this straight-forward announcement and to choose and arrange the incidents in the story so they suggest, rather than state, the idea.

6. Keep to a consistent point of view. You could write this narrative from the point of view of the mouse, the cat, or an ironic observer with a sense of humor. The point of view is vital to the story, and it must be consistent. Changing the point of view will confuse your reader and destroy the effect of the story.

Exercises for Writing

1. Your main assignment for this section has already been given: write a full account of what happened with the cat and the mouse. Follow the guidelines for writing narratives given on pages 175 and 176.

2. Select any picture in this book that you feel contains a character or characters and situation that provide a good basis for a short story. Write a story using the picture as a basis for it.

3. Find two pictures of animals in this book. Use these two animals as a basis for a fable. Your story should have a moral at the end that states a truth about human nature in one sentence. This, of course, is the main point or theme of the story.

176

On Your Own

1. Find an incident in a recent newspaper that is dramatic. Write a story based upon the incident.

2. Find a dramatic picture containing good material for a story. Write a story based upon the picture.

3. Describe two people you know. Use these two characters as a basis for a story. Create a problem for them and tell the story of the conflict and its resolution.

Summary

Effective storywriters read many stories by other writers. Through wide reading they gain a feeling for the narrative structure of a story. They notice how a good writer hooks the reader's interest quickly by involving believable characters in a dramatic situation.

Remember that an effective storywriter stimulates the reader to turn to the next page to read more. Read stories and novels. Try to analyze how the authors create their characters and plunge them into situations where problems need solutions. How do they motivate you to want to read further? Meanwhile, practice by writing stories of your own. You will learn more about storywriting with each attempt. Do not become discouraged. Merely reading about writing or talking about it will not help you to write well. You will learn to write through writing more. As Epictetus said, "If you wish to be a writer, write."

A hard beginning maketh a good ending.
—John Heywood

The
Unexpected
18

As you look at what people are doing, and hear what they are saying, and observe what is happening around you, search for surprises — for things you have never heard of before, or for unusual variations on familiar things. Out of such observation comes some of the best material for writing.

All of these pictures dramatize an important similarity between photography and composition. The weakest performances in each medium are often thoughtless, trite repetitions of what has been done a thousand times before. Two classic examples are snapshots at the seashore and trips last summer. Whereas these are generally dull, it is the fresh, unexpected touch that adds zest to your work.

Exercises for Writing

1. Write a story (a fantasy, if you like) that uses the image on page 186 as a central point.

2. Write a description of the effect on your thinking or feeling of the picture on page 187.

3. Write a composition or story that will explain the situation pictured on page 188 and make it believable.

4. Study the picture on page 189. Use this character and image as the basis for a story.

5. What do you think of the picture on page 190? Write a brief composition explaining your reaction to it.

6. Write a composition on the quotation below. Think of an experience in your past that this quotation illustrates.

It is the unforeseen, the unexpected, that always happens.
—Latin Proverb

187

On Your Own

1. Write a visually sharp description of a surprise you have experienced in the past.

2. Write a character sketch of the most surprising individual you have ever met.

3. Select a television show or radio show or movie that had an unexpected ending. Explain how the writer achieved the unexpected effect.

4. Jokes usually depend upon how unexpected the punch line is. Write a good joke (in good taste) that you have heard which has a good, unexpected punch line.

Summary

Using "the unexpected" in writing a story or a composition can have a fresh effect upon the reader. The device must be used with care, however. Unexpected events or situations have to be believable — not merely thrown in for effect. One of the dullest, most over-used devices is to have the character in a terrifying situation wake up and realize, "It was only a dream." Never use this device. Always make the unexpected seem logical to the reader, or you will lose your reader and your credibility as a writer.

> *But mount to paradise*
> *By the stairway of surprise.*
> —Ralph Waldo Emerson

Developing the
Imagination

In this section, the subject is imagination. It is a quality that often distinguishes the best writing done by both amateurs and professionals.

Although imaginative writing is usually fiction, it is also useful for developing ideas. Since not all ideas can be made clear by visible, factual evidence, a writer can be very convincing by using an imaginative conception to develop an idea. An example might be starting with real evidence then imagining what lies behind it. One author, Judy Syphers, used imagination to make a point by titling an essay, "Why I Want a Wife."

It is possible for you to study these pictures in a literal way, trying to figure out just exactly what was happening when the photographer clicked the shutter or the artist manipulated his material. Then you can write a technically satisfying explanation. The real purpose of this section, however, is to stir up your imagination. The pictures were chosen to lead you to create ideas, images, and places so that what you communicate is not what can be proved but what you see in your imagination.

If you get stuck, consider these questions and ideas:

- Does the scene remind you of an analogy?

- What is the spirit of the picture?

- Is there an essential conflict or contrast in the picture?

- How are the parts of the image related?

- Invent a scene of which the picture could have been a part.

- Is an abstract idea suggested?

- What is suggested by the shapes and forms?

- Write a silly explanation.

- Create an imaginative title for a picture.

Edgar Allan Poe is a good example of a writer whose imagination led him to create significant forms of literature. He invented the detective story and also established the short story as a fixed form of literature. In fact, it was through writing detective stories that he perfected the short story form. He proceeded to lay down definite prescriptions for the writing of short stories. The writer, he said, should conceive "a certain single *effect*," and all the incidents in the story should combine to create this effect. "If his very first sentence tend not to the out-bringing of this effect, then in his very first step, he has committed a blunder," says Poe. In the short story, "a picture is at length painted which leaves in the mind of him who contemplates it with a kindred art, a sense of the fullest satisfaction."

Exercises for Writing

1. Create an imaginative title for each picture, pages 195-198.

2. Write an imaginative story or essay based on the picture on page 195.

3. Write an imaginative essay or story that uses the picture on page 196 as its basic point.

4. Write an imaginative composition about the character in the picture on page 197.

5. Write an imaginative, descriptive essay explaining what the sculpture on page 198 represents.

198

Interior Monologues

All the following pictures here have been chosen for two kinds of exercises: (1) writing a first-person account of what a character seems to be thinking, either about himself or someone in the same scene; and (2) relating your own thoughts as you study a picture, or as you imagine yourself taking part in the scene.

This kind of writing is known as an interior monologue. It is also known as "stream-of-consciousness" writing. In an interior monologue, the character is talking with himself or herself; the thoughts are shared with readers. This type of writing is not as strict and orderly as a carefully composed piece of writing because thoughts do not usually come to a person in an organized way.

Here is an example of an interior monologue:

> Five minutes to go—the most important test I've ever taken. The head in front of me is bowed, just like mine. It's hot in here, but I feel like an iceberg—yeah, an iceberg that sunk the Titanic. Will I go down like the Titanic and not get the college I want? Waiting, waiting, waiting—talk about suspense! All the homework, the math they tried to pour into me—all the reading and writing—this is the bottom line, and I don't know anything. Nothing! My mind's an enormous blank screen. I can't even add 2 and 2. This is the bottom line—no faking it this time—no sweet smile and no excuse to cover up. For keeps! I become a number. My brain's a cucumber. The silence is heavy; I can even hear the hum of the electric clock. Here it comes—booklet, scratch paper, now or never. Sorry Miss Jones, sorry everybody. I wish I'd studied more. This is it! Well, good luck to me . . .

Whenever you write an interior monologue based upon a picture, be sure to select thoughts and feelings that are related to the general impression the picture conveys.

> *Write down the thoughts of the moment. Those that come unsought for are commonly the most valuable.*
> —Francis Bacon

Exercises

1. Write a fantasy about the picture on page 201 from the point of view of the house.

2. For the picture on page 202, write a composition involving the thoughts of the dog and the parking meter officer.

3. Use your imagination for the picture on page 203. What data may the computer be transmitting?

4. Write the thoughts of the unusual creature in the picture on page 204.

5. Study the picture on page 205. Decide who the character is and what she is thinking. Write down the thoughts that are going through her mind.

6. Study the picture on page 206. What are the thoughts of the person in the picture?

> *To know is nothing at all; to imagine is everything.*
> —Anatole France

> *Keep a good tongue in your head.*
> —Shakespeare

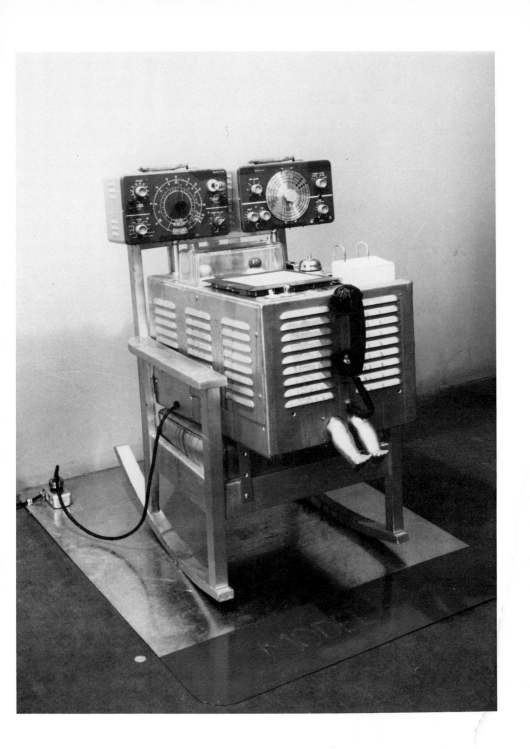

204

On Your Own

1. Imagine you have three days to live. Write a composition on how you would spend your three days.

2. Imagine that a friend has turned you into one of the following:

    a. a dog

    b. a fly

    c. a lion

Write a composition describing one day in your new life. Include both your thoughts and your actions.

3. Imagine you could be any historical figure in the past. Write a composition describing your thoughts and actions during one day as this person.

4. Imagine that you could travel anywhere in the world for one day. Where would you go and what would you do there?

5. Imagine that you have won ten million dollars in a contest and had to spend it all in one week. Write a composition on how you would spend the money. Be specific.

Summary

Imagination literally means image-making, creating pictures in the mind. The effective writer is always exploring and imagining, asking the question, "What if . . . ?" and playing the game of Let's Pretend. Use your imagination to the fullest when you write creatively, even though you base the writing on reality.

> *Imagination, not invention, is the supreme master*
> *of the art of life.*
> —Joseph Conrad

The Essay
20

In this section you will be asked to use the skills you have learned to write an essay. An essay is a composition that usually reflects the point of view of the author.

An essay may be written about any subject that interests the writer. In this case, you will study pictures from the city and pictures from the country. After examining the pictures, you must decide what main idea (thesis statement) you wish to develop, based upon these city and country scenes.

Exercises for Writing

Write a fully developed essay based on the following sets of pictures. These pictures depict various city and country scenes. Follow this procedure for writing your essay.

1. Write a detail list for each picture.

2. After you have written your detail list, decide what each picture suggests to you and write the main idea of the picture in one sentence.

3. Study the pictures involving the city. What similarities can you find? What contrasts? Use your detail list and main idea sentences to help you to discover what you want to say about city life.

4. Study the pictures from the country. Use your detail list and main idea sentences to help you to decide what you want to say about country life.

5. In your essay, you will compare and contrast city life and country life. Write a thesis sentence (main idea) which expresses the main idea you have formed about the similarities and differences between city life and country life. This will be the major theme and direction of your essay.

6. Decide what main points you wish to make that will develop and support your opinion about life in these two areas. Then construct a logical plan that your writing will follow.

7. Begin your essay with an introductory paragraph that uses your thesis sentence to give the reader a clear idea of what main point your essay will develop.

8. The body of your essay should move smoothly from one major point to the next, using details, illustrations and evidence to support your thoughts.

9. The final paragraph should sum up your thesis statement and restate it in a clear, forceful way.

10. The most important factor to remember before you write about any subject is to know clearly what you want to say before you write. If you think clearly and know what main points you want to develop to support the thesis statement of the essay, the writing should flow smoothly.

11. Give your essay an interesting title that suggests the thesis.

Writing your essay well will demand close observation, careful thought, and the application of many of the skills you have learned. Do not be satisfied with a first draft. After you have written your first draft, read it aloud to yourself and make changes that will improve the essay. Then give it to a friend for his or her critical reactions. Finally, revise as necessary for clarity, completeness, and accuracy.

214

216

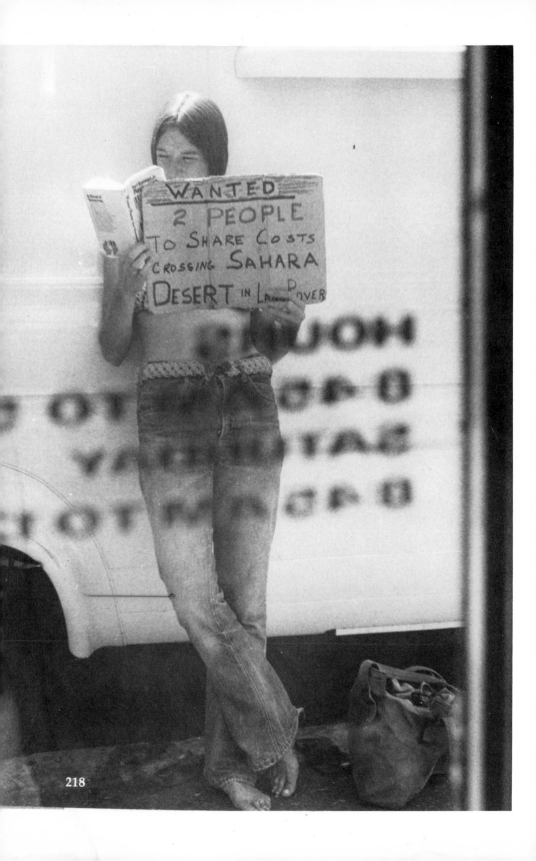

219

220

駐車場入口

222

On Your Own

If you have completed the sections and assignments in this book, you have worked hard. You are now truly on your own with the writing process. Your skills of observation and interpretation should be sharper and more perceptive. Your sense of emphasis, your use of imagery, and your sense of organization should have improved. You should also feel more fluent and comfortable when writing imaginatively.

As you continue to write and practice the skills you have learned, heed the definition of Mary Heaton Vorse: "The art of writing is the art of applying the seat of the pants to the seat of the chair." And then writing, of course. Remember the Chinese proverb:

I hear and I forget.
I see and I remember.
I do and I understand.

Good luck and write well!

Hart Day Leavitt
David A. Sohn

Photo Credits and Captions

Page

2. A teacher faces a young student — and he faces her — in an intimate moment of wonderment. *Bruce Roberts, Photo Researchers*

3. An Italian house painter gets instructions. *Hart Leavitt*

4. A 9th grade student listens. *Hart Leavitt*

4. These players obey the rule: Keep your eye on the ball. *Dale Guldan*

9. Spectators in Vienna watch a military parade. *Yoichi R. Okamoto*

10. This modern Belgian painter creates disconnected, impossible, satiric, and sometimes symbolic pictures. *Painting by Rene Magritte, "The Blank Signature," from the collection of Mr. and Mrs. Paul Mellon*

11. The Las Vegas "strip," one of the most famous alleys of entertainment in America. *Photo courtesy of Las Vegas Chamber of Commerce*

12. This artist says his pictures are "serious games." *Graphic drawing by M. C. Escher, "Relativity," Museum of Modern Art, New York*

18. The winner parades after the bullfight. *Jenaro Olivares*

19. This photograph of a film company making a movie was taken on a street in Rome. *Hart Leavitt*

20. Three hopeful young actresses wait in the wings at a professional school for child actors. *Suzanne Szasz*

21. This American artist painted more than 150 different versions of this imaginary scene in order to dramatize his faith in the harmony of nature. *Painting by Edward Hicks, "Peaceable Kingdom," Brooklyn Museum of Art, New York*

22. This is a stunt picture of a lion being dragged into a car wash. *James Hamilton*

27. These skeletons of a man and an ape were part of a scientific exhibit at a Toronto museum. *Hart Leavitt*

28. An elephant is transported to the next stop in a traveling circus. *Jill Freedman, Archives Pix, New York*

29. Charles Deaton designed this experimental house to fit into the contours and atmosphere of a natural setting in Arizona. *Photo courtesy of Charles Deaton, architect*

30. The photographer caught the moment when one boxer delivered "a right hook to the chops." *Sven-Gosta Johansson*

36. A woman stops for a snack in a supermarket restaurant in Tokyo. *Hart Leavitt*

37. The one-arm bandit wins again. *Elliot Erwitt, Magnum*

38. More than 1,000 runners cross a 7-mile bridge in Marathon, Florida, in an annual race over the length of the bridge. *Associated Press*

39. A group of Italian students practice diplomacy with an American photographer. *Hart Leavitt*

40. Freezing rain decorates New England elms. *Hart Leavitt*

46. Spanish bullfighter executes the "Manclentina Pass." *Peter Buckley*

47. Star English soccer goalie trains his son. *Mike Hollist*

48. Horses fighting. *Gunnar Cornelius*

49. The photographer strapped his camera between the train rails and tripped the shutter by remote control. *Robert Michel*

50. Trombone player in a jazz band. *Richard Graber*

51. High school hurdlers compete in New England track meet. *Wendy Maeda,* Boston Globe

57. Two men plan a business deal. *Hart Leavitt*

58. Nurse takes a coffee break. *Carl Perutz*

59. A Geisha girl shows her style. *David Linton*

60. ". . . and the pitcher comes out of her wind-up . . ." *John Avery*

61. ". . . and the pitcher comes of his wind-up . . ." *Photo courtesy of Chicago White Sox*

62. Counsellor comforts boy at camp for disturbed children. *Suzanne Szasz*

63. A little girl in a crowd needs help. *Hart Leavitt*

64. This picture dramatizes the great French photographer's philosophy of taking pictures at what he describes as "the decisive moment." *Henri Cartier-Bresson, Magnum*

65. A boy lifts off at the beach. *Lou Bernstein*

71. A Henry Moore sculpture doesn't interest this young boy. *Hart Leavitt*

72. The artist suggests joy and movement in her creation. *Sculpture by Dorothy Robbins, "The Dancing Bride"*

73. The photographer caught this pose by the winner of a Florida "Man of the Month" contest. *Dick Falcon*

74. A still picture from Charlie Chaplin's classic comedy "Shoulder Arms." *Photo courtesy Museum of Modern Art, New York*

75. An American paratrooper loaded with gear and hardware for D-Day in 1945. *Robert Capa, Magnum*

76. The artist's personal interpretation of the famous actress, painted in 1954. *Painting by William de Kooning, "Marilyn" Courtesy, Collection of Roy Newberger*

77. *One of a series of public relations photos of Marilyn Monroe.*

84. Music has charms to sooth a savage beast
   Or soften rocks, or bend a knotted oak.
                              — William Congreve
   Rene Maltete

85. The Rudi Lenz Chimps imitate a jazz band in their circus act. *Associated Press*

86. Trio for three telephones. *Hart Leavitt*

87. The art of makeup. *Annemarie Heinrich*

88. A seal takes a sun break at the New England Aquarium. *Hart Leavitt*

91. Another invented image by the photographic magician, who is a master of darkroom tricks. *Jerry Uelsmann*

92. The author took this picture because it suggested these
   lines from de la Mare's poem "The Listeners":
       For he suddenly smote upon the door, even
       Louder, and lifted his head: —
       "Tell them I came and no one answered,
           That I kept my word," he said.
   Hart Leavitt

93. Images suggested by rock formations in Arizona. *Hart Leavitt*

94. *Cartoon by Gaham Wilson. Courtesy of the artist.*

95. The artist painted this picture after visiting a nightclub for teenagers. *Painting by the South American artist Ernest Grau, "La Espera"*

96. A lithograph. *Matt Sohn, "Eyes, Eyes"*

103. Japanese umpires come to America to learn to "call 'em as they see 'um" at a school for baseball arbiters. *Steve Dozier*

104. "Woman's work is never done," especially for a young mother. *Suzanne Szasz*

105. Girl reading. *Hart Leavitt*

106. The title suggests the spirit of almost any bureaucratic office where one has to wait in line. *Painting by George Tooker, "Government Bureau," Metropolitan Museum of Art, New York*

107. Reflection of a skyscraper in New York in the windows of the CBS building. *Hart Leavitt*

108. Desert sand dune. *William Garnett*

114. The famous American artist gives precise meaning to the old cliché, "bird's eye view." *Painting by Andrew Wyeth, "Soaring," Shelburne (Vermont) Museum*

115. . . . and a photographer reverses the perspective. *Hart Leavitt*

116. A traveler rests on the steps of the Acropolis. *Hart Leavitt*

117. . . . and another photographer gives meaning to another cliché, "worm's eye view." *Ross Lewis*

118. The great French photographer catches a group at a decisive moment of tension. *Henri Cartier-Bresson, Magnum*

124. Russian and American soldiers meet after the defeat of the Nazis in World War II. *United States Department of Defense*

125. A sailor waits. *Hart Leavitt*

126. A fly takes five. *Hart Leavitt*

127. An imaginative creation of the spirit of the nuclear age. *Drawing by Fons van Woerkum*

132. A London "character" catches up on the late news in Trafalgar Square. *Hart Leavitt*

133. "Mummy, I'm all through!" *Suzanne Szasz*

134. Sometimes the ostrich does NOT have its head in the sand. *Michael Lichterman, Scholastic Magazine photo contest*

135. Monkey apes the man of fashion. *David Linton*

136. Many artists have played games with the old masters. *Painting by Fernand Otero, "Mona Lisa, age 12," Museum of Modern Art, New York*

137. Quick relief for a headache. *Hart Leavitt*

138. Time for a catnap. *Thomas Friedman, Photo Researchers*

143. Police capture a murderer. *Winfield Parks, Jr., Providence Journal*

144. This editorial drawing symbolizes international conflict. *Robert Pryor,* New York Times

145. Male striker in England argues with a woman. *Don McPhee*

146. Graduation day tension. *Hart Leavitt*

147. A Frenchwoman is accused of collaborating with the Nazis during World War II. *Henry Cartier-Bresson, Magnum*

148. The photographer entitled this "Boy with Gun." *George W. Gardner*

154. In 1951, as Commander of the United States Military Forces, President Truman fired Gen. Douglas MacArthur for disobeying an order of the Joint Chiefs of Staff. Gen. Eisenhower, one of the Chiefs, reacts on hearing the news. *United Press International*

155. This famous American painting may or may not be satiric. *Painting by Grant Wood, "American Gothic" Art Institute of Chicago*

156. This is one shot in a picture story about a boy who is deaf and dumb. *Gary Parker*

157. One of a series of poses of a fashion model. *Jules Alexander*

158. This scene was photographed at a fashionable horse race in France. *Jeanloup Sieff*

159. Hispanics at the U.N. *Hart Leavitt*

160. Woman cadet, a graduate of paratroop training, takes charge of a platoon of West Point plebes. *Steve Auchard,* The New Jersey Record

161. This is one of a series in a picture story about athletics in a small town in Kansas. *Jim Richardson*

162. Mother and daughter. *Arthur Tress*

167. These two statues, photographed on the island of Mykonos, are said to be in honor of Antony and Cleopatra. *Hart Leavitt*

168. This is one of a series of pictures of two students in a lively conversation on the campus of a large university. *Hart Leavitt*

169. Another version of the eternal triangle. *Anthony Bruculere*

170. Friendly rivalry during annual soccer game between men and women at Old Leigh regatta in Scotland. (The men lost.) *John Jones*

171. A young Italian couple talk things over on a street in Rome. *Hart Leavitt*

177.- All of these pictures were taken by the author in his kitchen after
182. the cat found the mouse. *Hart Leavitt*

186. A bike rider in Europe decorates his machine with a sense of irony. *Hart Leavitt*

187. The skier takes a coffie break. *Hart Leavitt*

188. This is an elaborately contrived photograph mimicking the style of the famous Spanish painter Salvador Dali, who is shown suspended in the picture, along with the cats. *Philippe Halsman*

189. A high school student made up this image for an assignment to create a bizarre picture based on the abstract paintings of Piet Mondrian. *Drawing by Dan Kent*

190. A small girl hams it up in Vigelund Park in Oslo. *Hart Leavitt*

195. This is a photograph of a farmer in Europe walking through his garden. *Robert Hausser*

196. The author took this picture on impulse. When it was enlarged, the pieces fit together in an interesting way. *Hart Leavitt*

197. This is a picture of the back of a girl who has just been swimming. *David X. Young*

198. The English artist creates a symbol of the nuclear age. *Henry Moore sculpture, Courtesy Art Institute of Chicago.*

201. Another work of darkroom magic by the inventive American photographer. *Jerry Uelsmann*

202. "Who, ME?" *Ian Torrance,* Scottish Daily Record

203. Technically, this work is called a "Moter-driven assemblage: aluminum painted rocking chair, metal case, two instrument boxes with dials, plastic case containing yellow and blue lights, panel with number, bell, 'rocker switch', pack of index cards, directions for operation, light switch, telephone receiver, doll's legs." *Construction by Edward Kienholz, "The Friendly Grey Computer — Star Gauge Model No. 54," Museum of Modern Art, New York*

204. *Pablo Picasso, "Baboon and Young," Museum of Modern Art, New York*

205. A young actress playing the part of the deaf-mute in *The Fantastics.* *Hart Leavitt*

206. A young girl was photographed against a window. *Helena Kolda Duchacek*

211. Three boys show off for the photographer in Philadelphia. *Hart Leavitt*

212. Western farmer checks a building to see if it will last through the winter. *Kevin Manning*

213. This photograph of a New York skyscraper was deliberately moved in the process of enlarging it. *Hart Leavitt*

214. A woman sweeps the street in Japan. *Hart Leavitt*

215. Street musician in Boston. *Hart Leavitt*

216. A shephard does his work in England. *Gerald Lacey*

217. Display window in a shop of high fashion in Rome. *Hart Leavitt*

218. Girl traveler advertises for help in Rome. *Hart Leavitt*

219. Russian peasants enjoy Saturday night at local club. *Henri Cartier-Bresson, Magnum*

220. Traveling in Roumania. *Hart Leavitt*

221. River fishing in France. *Hart Leavitt*

222. Circus hand washes down an elephant in Tokyo. *Hart Leavitt*

223. Owner tries to persuade bull at country fair. *Hart Leavitt*

224. Peaceful scene along canal in France. *Hart Leavitt*

LANGUAGE ARTS BOOKS

Tandem: Language in Action Series
Point/Counterpoint, *Dufour and Strauss*
Action/Interaction, *Dufour and Strauss*

Business Communication
Business Communication Today!,
 Thomas and Fryar
Successful Business Writing, *Sitzmann*
Successful Business Speaking, *Fryar
 and Thomas*
Successful Interviewing, *Sitzmann and
 Garcia*
Successful Problem Solving, *Fryar and
 Thomas*
Working in Groups, *Ratliffe and Stech*
Effective Group Communication,
 Ratliffe and Stech

Reading
Reading by Doing, *Simmons and Palmer*
Literature Alive, *Gamble and Gamble*
Building Real Life English Skills, *Penn
 and Starkey*
Practical Skills in Reading, *Keech and
 Sanford*
Essential Life Skills Series, *Penn and
 Starkey*

Grammar
Grammar Step-By-Step Vol. 1, *Pratt*
Grammar Step-By-Step Vol. 2, *Pratt*

Speech
Getting Started in Public Speaking,
 Prentice and Payne
Listening by Doing, *Galvin*
Person to Person, *Galvin and Book*
Person to Person, Workbook, *Galvin
 and Book*
Speaking by Doing, *Buys, Sills and Beck*
Self-Awareness, *Ratliffe and Herman*
Literature Alive, *Gamble and Gamble*
Contemporary Speech, *Hopkins and
 Whitaker*
Creative Speaking, *Buys et al.*

Journalism
Journalism Today!, *Ferguson and Patten*

Media
Understanding Mass Media, *Schrank*
The Mass Media Workbook, *Hollister*
Media, Messages & Language, *McLuhan,
 Hutchon and McLuhan*
Understanding the Film, *Johnson and
 Bone*
Photography in Focus, *Jacobs and
 Kokrda*
Televising Your Message, *Mitchell and
 Kirkham*

Theatre
Dynamics of Acting, *Snyder and
 Drumstra*
Play Production Today!, *Beck et al.*
Acting and Directing, *Grandstaff*
An Introduction to Theatre and Drama,
 Cassady and Cassady
The Book of Scenes for Acting Practice,
 Cassady

Mythology
Mythology and You, *Rosenberg and
 Baker*
World Mythology: A Collection of Great
 Myths and Epics, *Rosenberg*

Mystery and Science Fiction
The Detective Story, *Schwartz*
You and Science Fiction, *Hollister*

Writing and Composition
Lively Writing, *Schrank*
Snap, Crackle & Write, *Schrank*
An Anthology for Young Writers,
 Meredith
Writing in Action, *Meredith*
Writing by Doing, *Sohn and Enger*
The Art of Composition, *Meredith*
Look, Think & Write!, *Leavitt and Sohn*
The Book of Forms for Everyday Living,
 Rogers

For further information or a current catalog, write:
National Textbook Company
4255 West Touhy Avenue
Lincolnwood, Illinois 60646-1975 U.S.A.